CHASING STEAM IN 1966

When travelling out of Marylebone on the 14.38 Nottingham Victoria train on a Monday to Friday, one could observe, here at Rugby Central, the locomotive working that day's 17.20 Nottingham starter. If she was, as in this case on Monday, 13 June, a 'requirement' (as Banbury's 44860 was) I alighted there to catch it.

CHASING STEAM IN 1966

A Teenager in Pursuit of the Disappearing Steam Locomotive

KEITH WIDDOWSON

The History Press

Cover illustrations: Front: A run-past featuring 0-6-0ST WD196 *Errol Lonsdale*; *Back:* Jinty 47202 fitted with condensation equipment for tunnel working in London.

First published 2024

The History Press
97 St George's Place, Cheltenham,
Gloucestershire, GL50 3QB
www.thehistorypress.co.uk

© Keith Widdowson, 2024

The right of Keith Widdowson to be identified as the Author
of this work has been asserted in accordance with the
Copyright, Designs and Patents Act 1988.

British Library Cataloguing in Publication Data.
A catalogue record for this book is available from the British Library.

ISBN 978 1 80399 519 9

Typesetting and origination by The History Press
Printed and bound in Great Britain by TJ Books Limited, Padstow, Cornwall.

Trees for LYfe

CONTENTS

ABOUT THE AUTHOR

Keith Widdowson was born at St Mary Cray, Kent, and having attended the nearby schools of Poverest and Charterhouse commenced his forty-five-year career with British Railways in June 1962. Including locations such as Waterloo, Cannon Street, Wimbledon, Crewe, Euston, Blackfriars, Paddington and Croydon, most of it was spent diagramming locomotive and train crews.

After spending several years in London, Crewe and Sittingbourne, he returned to his roots in 1985, where he met Joan, with whom he had a daughter, Victoria – and he recently became a grandfather to Darcey. Having had several books published on his travels in both the UK and Europe, he spends time gardening, writing articles for railway magazines and is a member of both the local residents' association and the Sittingbourne & Kemsley Light Railway.

INTRODUCTION

The year 1966 was dominated by the lead-up to the winning and celebrations after England's triumph over West Germany in football's World Cup. While I'm not denying it was a historic event in MY world, a matter of greater importance was taking place – the demise of the steam locomotive. For over 100 years, the dominant power on Britain's railways was being discarded in favour of a more innovative, less labour-intensive diesel or electric-powered substitute.

I had joined British Railways (BR) in the June of 1962 and, I have to admit, I knew very little of the political machinations involved in attempting to turn around the heavy losses being incurred by this nationalised industry. My mother, God bless her, had picked up on my interest in timetable reading and wrote to BR asking if there was a job for me – my daily commute to school involved a bus journey and the need to understand the relevant schedules in order to arrive on time. As an aside, this fascination with timetables led to many outings with my younger brother, utilising either the Green or Red Rover tickets, which allowed unlimited travel on London Transport routes at week-ends – essential planning was needed, especially on the country routes, to avoid being stranded for hours. At this point, although I was never a trainspotter, I must confess to being the equivalent regarding London Transport buses.

Having passed the medical and clerical exams, I was allocated a position in the fourth-floor offices at Waterloo, in effect as the office gofer. This was, retrospectively, a wonderful initiation into the world of work. For sure, I made the tea, but I also ran errands for all and sundry all over the vast station. A perfect illustration of life back then is John Schlesinger's 1961 British Transport documentary film *Terminus* – depicting twenty-four hours in the everyday (and night) activities to be found under the cavernous roof.

I witnessed it all. From the West Indians arriving via Southampton as part of the *Windrush* generation; the shoe shine boys; the down and outs using the seats as overnight accommodation; the lengthy, winding queues under the triangular signs suspended from the roof for the Summer Saturday trains to holiday destinations, and the alcoholic aroma emanating from the Leake Street vaults, to visits to the station-announcer's panoramic periscope-like viewpoint just under the roof and making numerous trips to obtain as many 'freebies' as possible whenever a promotion (usually food orientated) stall was on the concourse; and finally, queuing, at the manager's behest, for first-day issues of postage stamps at the post office.

I was to be seen sunbathing during my lunch break next to the beehives on the roof – avoiding falling from the edge (without any guard rails) onto the extensive glass roof covering the concourse. I also made visits to the Bill Office, which was in the arches adjacent to Waterloo Road, to collect leaflets for excursions or cheap day offers. The manager there often gave me a copy of station posters depicting the latest tranche of closures – examples being Hurstbourne, New Romney and the Cowes and Ventnor sections of the Isle of Wight system.

Having sometime during 1964 been moved to a different office, I was 'awarded the honour' of setting up a tea urn on the 'Camping Coach'. This was to be positioned during off-peak hours at one of Waterloo's twenty-one platforms to promote the use of them to prospective customers – they were mainly located at several New Forest stations. 'So what?' you might say. Now, here's the thing. The coach was located in the North Sidings and was to be shunted via West Crossings to a platform. Having walked over to it before the move, I managed to obtain footplate rides from the friendly crews on a couple of Standard 3MT tanks and a West Country (WC) smooth-cased *Calstock*.

It may surprise readers to know that I was one of the rare species within the clerical grades who had joined the railways unaware of the associated travel perks. I was surrounded by clerks and managers, the majority of whom had specially joined BR to further their hobby utilising the free passes and reduced fares to travel the country taking photographs of closing lines and the disappearing steam locomotives.

Slowly but surely, the addiction began to take hold. Initially visiting lines threatened under the 1963 Beeching axe, the majority of which were still steam operated, I began, from the March of 1964, to document my travels. Following each outing, I transferred information that I had gleaned and scribbled down in my accompanying travel-worn notebooks into an A4-sized diary. Without this foresight, books such as this could never have been compiled, the minutiae of each journey being far too great to be drawn out of my memory bank.

A regular stroll around Waterloo Station, having had lunch in the staff canteen adjacent to Platform 15, included a visit to the country end of the lengthy Platform 11, to admire the preparations involved for the usually Merchant Navy (MN)-powered 13.30 Weymouth departure. The steam locomotive, I came to appreciate over the years, is a temperamental animal. She must be treated with respect for the crew to obtain the best out of her. Often in a worn-out and rundown condition, and covered in grease and oil, these unpredictable beasts required multi-skilled crews whose talents still, to this day, amaze me. The intoxicating aroma associated with these iron horses still sends shivers down my spine and, on the rare occasions these days of obtaining a run with one that I've never travelled with, the orgasmic euphoria stays with me for days afterwards.

As this book deals specially with the year 1966, I will now bring the reader up to speed as to where I was within the BR employment hierarchy. I was unsure as to which way my career was heading. Having been bored senseless by attending an evening class dedicated to progression within the ticket offices, I switched to a Rules & Signalling evening class, which was held in the Mutual Improvement Class (MIC) room above Clapham Junction Station.

Regrettably failing to comprehend the importance of understanding block sections and semaphore signals – and citing the fact that the future lay in coloured light signals – the lure of a Tuesday night trip on the 'Kenny Belle' (a sobriquet bestowed on this unadvertised service by enthusiasts) to get me there from my Cannon Street office morphed into diverting to Waterloo for the 18.00 and 18.09 steam departures. At least the Cannon Street job, involving journal marking, performance statistics and analysis of train running, gave me an increased income, thus allowing me to travel on numerous rail tours that year.

That November, having obtained further promotion within the clerical grades with a position at Wimbledon, I was to finally achieve job satisfaction: that of locomotive and train crew diagramming, which was to see me through most of my career within the railway industry. By 1966, I had morphed from a track-basher, racing around the country to travel over as many doomed lines as possible, to a haulage-basher intent on catching runs with as many steam locomotives as possible.

To those who have purchased this book without realising what terminology such as the frequently used 'required' means, let me explain. While *any* run behind a steam locomotive was welcomed, the addictive obsession of obtaining a run with a locomotive that I had never travelled with before (and therefore was 'required') was a haulage-basher's objective – the capture being euphorically red-lined in whatever dog-eared Ian Allan *Locoshed* book was the current issue.

To this end, as can be read within the first couple of paragraphs of this tome, the Southern Region allocation was homed in on. Following that completion, I spread my wings throughout the UK mainland, coming across many like-minded devotees from many parts of the country. Upon such meet-ups, information (don't forget, it was in pre-Internet days where any publishable information was not seen until months after the event) was readily exchanged as to which trains remained steam-hauled, which had succumbed to diesel, what sheds were closing, etc. This was where the camaraderie came to the fore. We came from all walks of life, not all being railwaymen and therefore not all enjoying the travel perks such as mine. There again, with no automatic barriers and less-frequent ticket checks, who cared?

I had missed the King and Castle classes out of Paddington; I had missed the School classes out of Charing Cross; I had missed the Brits out of Liverpool Street; I had missed the Duchesses out of Euston; I had missed the Gresley Pacifics out of King's Cross; I had missed the Scots and Jubilees out of St Pancras and so I was left with the scraps. Hitler's forces had incarcerated my father in a prisoner-of-war camp for many years, otherwise I would have perhaps been born earlier, but it is what it is. I made, albeit belatedly, the best of it and here is the result.

It was sad to see the steam locomotive in its death throes but, somewhat selfishly, I'm glad I witnessed it. It was a slightly ghoulish hobby, being in at the end of the giants of the Industrial Revolution; after all, we teenagers were never going to get old – we were going to live forever and getting old was a lifetime away. Well, here it is now.

Ironically, courtesy of people such as Dai Woodham, the steam locomotive will outlive us all. The burgeoning number of preservation societies with their dedicated bunch of volunteers have saved over 300 examples for future generations to enjoy. Well done them!

Another plus over recent years is the acceptance of trainspotting as an eccentricity not to be ashamed of – TV programmes featuring Chris Tarrant,

Michael Portillo and Dan Snow have furthered the cause. Then again, with *The Flying Scotsman* centenary celebrations in 2023, she was never out of the news.

A concerted effort was made by this teenaged author in love with steam to obtain runs behind as many of them as the monies (of a junior clerk) would permit. With financial responsibilities such as mortgages/debts and the distraction of the opposite sex yet to kick in, the world, as I saw it, was my oyster. All corners of the BR network that still retained passenger trains hauled by the fast-diminishing iron horse were visited. The last runs of disappearing classes on closing railway lines – all were in the mix.

With more and more routes having just overnight mail trains powered by steam, fifty-seven nights that year were spent away from the comfort of a warm bed. Here, the reader will find the results of that frenzied time. The disappointments caused by unanticipated diesel locomotives (DLs) turning up; the euphoria of an unexpected catch; and the comradeship (and rivalry) among like-minded colleagues. Statistically, my achievements that year are contained in the appendices.

For readers who were not around during that pivotal year, here's what you missed. For those who were there, enjoy your own special memories.

JANUARY

A COLD COMMUTE
WATERLOO, WOKING & WESSEX

London's Waterloo Station was opened by the London & South Western Railway (L&SWR) in 1848, replacing the original terminus of the line from Southampton at Nine Elms, a less than convenient location for customers requiring central London. Initially named Waterloo Bridge, in the never-to-be-realised hope of an extension further into London, the somewhat piecemeal disorder of buildings that had developed over the intermediate years were extensively rebuilt, with the Victory Arch to commemorate the fallen of the First World War being encompassed in 1922.

Woking (originally Common until 1843) was opened in 1838 as a station on the Nine Elms to Winchfield line, with the tracks being quadrupled in 1904 and electrified in 1937. Basingstoke was opened in 1840 upon completion of the route between London and Southampton – Great Western Railway's (GWR) broad-gauge arrived in 1848, with L&SWR's route to Salisbury completing the scene in 1857.

As mentioned within the Introduction, during the previous year I had raced around the country visiting closing lines and chasing classes of steam locomotives destined for the cutter's torch. Under my nose, however, on my home patch of the Southern Region (SR), the gradual rundown of the steam fleet was gathering pace. To this end, to travel with as many SR-allocated steam locomotives as possible before their annihilation, I began to catch runs out of Waterloo on the plethora of steam-worked departures during the evening rush hour.

The choice, at the beginning of 1966, was fantastic. Stopping services to Basingstoke/Salisbury departed at 17.09, 17.41, 18.09 and 18.54. As for the main line, although the 17.00 and 19.00 West of England departures had gone Warship-operated, the truncated 18.00 service at Salisbury retained steam – nearly always a sparkling clean 70E locomotive. Then there were the Bournemouth/Weymouth trains of 17.23 (FO), 17.30, 18.22 (FO) and 18.30 completing the scene. Returning trains were the 18.39 arrival (15.08 ex-Bournemouth Central), the 20.25 arrival (15.50 ex-Weymouth) and the 20.29 arrival (18.35 ex-Salisbury).

With no Total Operations Processing System (TOPS) available to us back then, on most evenings an assemblage of diehard haulage-bashers (I include myself among them) turned up at Waterloo and travelled out on whatever train sated their needs – i.e., something new for haulage or for mileage-accumulation purposes. There was always a friendly rivalry among us in being the first to obtain the 'magic' 1,000 miles behind as many different Bulleids as possible.

A review of one of my previous books highlighted that some steam-age reminiscence-orientated publications are overwhelmed with locomotive numbers, but that mine do not suffer from this. I will, therefore, use the numbers only when necessary, e.g. when caught for the very first occasion.

During the previous year, according to notes I made at the time, the 18.39 arrival into Waterloo was diagrammed for the Merchant Navy (MN) class, having gone down on the 08.30 that morning. I learnt, however, from a fellow gricer just before setting off on the 17.09 ex-Waterloo on Friday 7th, that it was now an Eastleigh duty and, sure enough, a grimy 'Flat', namely 34086 *219 Squadron*, turned up at Woking on it.

Never judge a book by its cover springs to mind here. She attained a respectable 74mph through Hersham with her eleven-coach, one-van train. With rumours circulating (subsequently proving false) that the MNs were to be replaced by Duchesses or Britannias, and personally still requiring six MNs, I would have somewhat selfishly preferred one of them that cold, frosty evening.

The following Monday (10th) saw me catch 35003 *Royal Mail* on the 17.30 departure – the returning trains from Basingstoke were noted as coming in covered in snow and ice. History shows that *Royal Mail* was to throw off the unkind sobriquet of 'Royal Snail' that had been given to it by us enthusiasts in the final weeks of SR steam – with several runs exceeding 100mph.

There were indeed numerous – and sometimes discourteous – monikers bandied around for the named locomotives: 'Sir Useless Missenden', 'Clapford' and 'Slime Regis' spring to mind. Seriously though, the names of faraway West Country destinations were an education to a London lad such as I. Was I ever to visit these places? As for the Battle of Britain names, although the somewhat repetitious squadron numbers were of little note, the Second World War chiefs of staff such as *Lord Dowding* and *Sir Keith Park*, or poignant names such as *Fighter Command* and *Spitfire*, sent some of us heading to our encyclopaedias on returning home to try to understand our British history.

More luck found me two days later, with *Belgian Marine* on the 17.30 and *Clovelly* on the returning 15.50 ex-Weymouth. As already mentioned, there was the wonderful choice of two steam trains with which to return from Basingstoke into Waterloo. To that end, I often alighted off the returning Bournemouth train at Woking in the hope of gaining yet another 'requirement' on the following Salisbury service – on this occasion, however, the power that night was Standard 5MT *Pendragon*, which I had already travelled with. Perhaps that was the excitement – the anticipation of not knowing for sure if a 'required' one was going to turn up – *but it might have*! These days, with certainty guaranteed courtesy of information gleaned off the Internet, the thrill of the catch, in my opinion, has perhaps been somewhat diluted.

The 17.30 Waterloo came up trumps once more on the 20th, with Light Pacific *Exeter* in charge. The train was full and standing-only as far as Woking where a special stop was made – the electric multiple unit (EMU) trains were in chaos due to the iced-up third rail. Although doing a double Woking that evening – i.e., into Waterloo on the 18.39 arrival and out again on the 18.54 (via the subway under the platforms to avoid ticket checks at the barriers) – no further locomotives were red-lined in my *Locoshed* book. Music wise, on that day, The Spencer Davis Group's 'Keep on Running' dislodged The Beatles' 'Day Tripper' from the number one spot, which it had held for the previous five weeks. No Christmas-orientated tunes back then!

Two further Standard 5MTs were 'scratched', or ticked off my list, on my next two outings. The Arthurian-named *King Leodegrance* worked the 17.09 departure on the 21st, while the same train on the 25th yielded a refugee from the Western Region (WR), namely 73037.

As an aside, many years later, having become a manager within the BR hierarchy, I was introduced to a senior manager who thought he recognised me from somewhere. Upon hearing he commuted from Farnborough, I realised (but feigned ignorance) that he was one of the occupants in the leading First Open carriage of the 17.09 train, who often shouted 'Clear orf out of here!' to miscreants such as myself who were leaning out of open windows listening to and recording the train's progress. With there often being a fair number of us in that leading coach, it wasn't unknown for the driver, having observed us hanging out of the windows en route, to offer footplate rides to us between the intermediate stations of Farnborough and Hook away from the prying eyes of officialdom, who were likely to be at Woking or Basingstoke. These offers were dealt with on a rotational basis and were eagerly accepted. Afterwards we would present ourselves, covered in coal dust and with blackened faces, to the wary landlord at a local Basingstoke pub for a pint and a wash.

My final jaunt in January was somewhat chaotic with the Warship DL on the 17.00 Waterloo to Exeter partially failing at Raynes Park and limping all the way to Basingstoke (departing Woking fifty-two minutes late), where it was substituted by steam. All the following services were heavily delayed – I was aboard the 73087 *Linette*-powered 17.09 Waterloo sustaining a twenty-six-minute-late arrival at Woking. For some undocumented reason, I loitered that night on Woking's platforms for almost two hours before returning, down-hearted at the power on the returning trains, into Waterloo. Only in recent years, to attend a reunion in a pub, have I ventured outside the station. With a preponderance of Scalextric-style roundabouts and demolition sites, I don't think I missed much.

Oh, how I was envious of those commuters enjoying steam train journeys to and from their workplaces. For sure, there were delays resulting from poor coal quality or inadequate boiler pressure due to the worn-out condition of the steam fleet, but didn't they realise it would all be gone in the not-too-distant future? I even worked with some of them – coming into the office, rubbing my nose in the fact that I had yet to catch a run with whatever locomotive they had enjoyed that morning.

Little did I know that following a promotional move to the Wimbledon office that November, my opportunity for a steam commute would be realised. Coming into Victoria from Kent, I then travelled via Clapham Junction to Wimbledon. If the Southeastern and Central Division trains behaved themselves by running to schedule, I could connect into the 08.16 Clapham Junction to Kensington (08.33 return) en route – thus allowing me to feel similarity on par with fellow gricers.

The off-peak, semi-fast Basingstoke stopping services out of Waterloo, departing at fifty-four minutes past each hour that were predominantly formed of a three- or four-vehicle formation were curtailed at Woking in the summer of 1965 timetable change – their replacement being formed of 'borrowed' WR diesel multiple units (DMUs). There was, however, one daytime departure out of Waterloo that remained steam operated. This was the 12.39 (SO): an anachronism that was a result of the fact that a Saturday morning duty was part and parcel of a working week back then. As for the remaining rush-hour departures, the first to fall was the 18.09, which went Class 33 DL and Trailer Control (TC) in December 1966. Just weeks later, the 17.41 Salisbury went EMU and terminated at Basingstoke. While the 17.09 finally succumbed to Class 33 DL haulage, in June 1967, just weeks before the end, the 18.54 remained steam hauled right up to the final Friday, 7 July.

BR Standard 4MT 76012 is captured storming away from Waterloo on Friday, 28 January with the 15.38 'Parcels' to Eastleigh. Until then, this 13-year-old had spent her whole life at Eastleigh. She was transferred to Guildford three months later, withdrawal coming that September.

Minutes earlier, and WC 34047 *Callington* had departed with the 15.35 semi-fast for Bournemouth Central. Just under a year later, while working the 10.08 York to Poole, the driver taking over at Eastleigh offered me a footplate ride with her to Southampton. With escaping steam leaking everywhere, thus obscuring vision across the footplate, the driver described the scenario as 'akin to a Chinese laundry', while notching up a bone-shaking 65mph in the darkness. What an experience!

FEBRUARY

THE SOMERSET & DORSET DIES
FAWLEY, BATH & BRIGHTON

The first five of fourteen outings that month saw me collect runs with the subsequently preserved *Blackmore Vale* (17.09 on 4 February) and, by waiting at Woking, the 73016 on the following 17.43 en route to Basingstoke. I returned that evening with *Croydon* on the five-coach, four-van Salisbury train. Having maxed at 78mph through Esher, she attained 66mph through Wimbledon despite the limit in from Raynes Park being 60mph before leaning sharply through the tightly curved platforms at Clapham Junction at an alarming angle. Many great runs were relished on this lightweight train over the coming months – the Nine Elms drivers were perhaps intent on giving us something to write about in the history books. The 18.09 supplied two of Guildford's Standard 5MTs later in that week while 'Spam Can' *Bude* worked the 17.43 on 10 February.

Friday, 11 February saw me head to the Hampshire branch of Fawley, which was to see its final passenger trains that day, having opened as late as 1925. Flush with money from a recent spell of overtime, I splashed out on a 3s 6d supplement to travel on the 'Bournemouth Belle'. This was my first non-stop run to Southampton Central. If my memory doesn't fail me, I think I also had a pot of tea. The Merchant 35003 *Royal Mail*-powered train, however, did at least attain 78mph down Winchester Bank with her ten Pullmans and one van; the curtain swinging and cutlery rattling made for a memorable trip.

Following an abortive visit to Lyndhurst Road on two New Forest stopping services, often a rich source for Eastleigh's Moguls and Standard Tanks,

Nine Elms Standard 3MT 82018 departs Clapham Junction with the 08.16 (unadvertised) train for Kensington (Olympia) on Monday, 7 February. She had spent the first ten years of her life at Exmouth Junction and was then dispatched to Nine Elms in 1962, having been displaced by dieselisation and line closures throughout the West Country. The signal box the train is about to pass under, West London Junction, had a protective steel roof placed over it during the Second World War, the 40-ton weight of which contributed to its subsidence the previous May. It was removed shortly afterwards.

Having just alighted at Wimbledon on Tuesday, 8 February, en route to my office workplace, the 07.27 Basingstoke to Waterloo came thundering through with double-chimneyed Standard 4MT 75075. This Swindon-built locomotive survived to the end of SR steam in July 1967.

Later that same day, one of the twenty Arthurian-named Standard 5MT's, 73117 Vivien, passes Wimbledon 'C' signal box with the 12.18 'Fairsky Boat Train' from Waterloo to Southampton Docks.

I was in place at Southampton for my first 'last train' encounter. The Fawley diesel-electric multiple unit (DEMU) was quite an experience with detonators[1] exploding on the route of the returning train (there were only two per day!), itself full and standing with enthusiasts. Alighting at Totton, I headed for the ticket office and purchased some souvenir tickets for Hythe and Fawley AFTER the last train had gone.

The following day (12th) saw me collect 206 steam miles by travelling to and from Leicester Central out of Marylebone. For several years, there were just three trains per day over this once-prestigious ex-Great Central Railway. Feted as the final British main line to be opened in 1899, the aspirations of the chairman Edward Watkin – who also had the South Eastern and Metropolitan Railways in his remit – of through-trains from the Midlands, under London and on to Europe was never realised. With island platforms, a ruling gradient

---

1   A railway detonator is a coin-sized device placed on the rail that is used as a loud warning to the train driver, usually indicating that there is a problem ahead. In this instance they were used in a non-celebratory way at the withdrawal of passenger trains over the line.

Having taken me over the Castleman's Corkscrew (Broadstone/Wimborne/Brockenhurst) route a week prior to its closure in April 1964, Bournemouth's Standard Mogul 76026 turned up again on Friday, 11 February, working the 13.57 Bournemouth Central to Southampton Terminus (a station that would be closing that September) – seen here departing Southampton Central.

Another scene at Southampton Central that February Friday was the 10.55 Plymouth to Brighton departure behind Weymouth's 73114 *Etarre*. She had taken over the train at Salisbury and was to survive just four more months.

I was in the area that day to travel on the second of the twice-daily, Monday to Friday DEMU services over the Fawley branch – passenger trains ceasing thereafter. Here at Fawley, the 15.46 from Eastleigh is seen after its arrival. This was my first 'last train' and the returning 16.48 departure was very crowded, setting off a series of detonators at the intermediate Frost Lane Crossing signal box en route. Although freight trains continued to serve the nearby Esso refinery for many years, there are plans (at the time of writing) for a reinstatement of passenger trains as far as Marchwood to cater for the expanding housing.

of 1 in 176 and a wider than usual loading gauge, had he received parliamentary approval and financial backing it could well have happened. As it was, the line settled down to provide regular fast expresses between London, Leicester and Nottingham in direct competition with the Midland Railway's trains out of St Pancras.

Also over this line, the famed fast 'Windcutter' freight trains ran between the Nottinghamshire coalfields and the middle England distribution centre of Woodford Halse. Regional changes in the late 1950s, however, saw the line fall into London Midland Region's hands and as such, they considered the route as being surplus to requirements. Dr Beeching's closure recommendations subsequently designated the line an unnecessary duplication. It was therefore left to wither and die.

However, to a steam enthusiast, the use of Stanier Black 5MTs, from a plethora of different sheds, on the four-coach trains was an addictive attraction.

For sure, some regular Colwick-allocated examples often monopolised the workings, but on this day, Tyseley's 44661 worked the returning 20.25 arrival into Marylebone.

One week later, while waiting for the same train at Aylesbury, it turned up running forty-seven minutes late, a replacement having been dispatched from Banbury and exchanged at Culworth Junction (south of Woodford Halse).

Britannias were drafted into Banbury for the Great Central (GC) services during the autumn of 1965, predominantly because of their greater tender capacity. Their reign lasted a mere three months and by the end of that year it was over, the main problem being that whenever failures requiring spare parts were needed, they had to be acquired from where the majority of the class had migrated to – Crewe or Carlisle – causing substantial periods out of service.

Although this new scenario was to provide a ready mix of Stanier 5MTs, with both the Banbury and Colwick foremen turning out visiting locomotives from a variety of sheds, I wasn't aware at the time that with Colwick having been transferred from the Eastern Region (ER) to London Midland Region (LMR), it was the recipient of twenty-six of the fittest Stanier 5MTs that had been displaced from elsewhere within the LMR purposely for the remaining GC line services.

It would have been repetitious to just sit and look out the window at the same scenery on each visit. The routine was to occupy the nearest empty compartment behind the locomotive, open the top light of the window to allow the smoke and steam to percolate and, with stopwatch to hand, record the train's progress while rarely being disturbed by other passengers or ticket collectors.

Once clear of the restraining Rickmansworth speed restriction, the drivers often let their machines off their leash. Being more used to the somewhat effeminate Bulleid exhaust, these Staniers let everyone around know they were coming, storming up the 1 in 105 climb to Amersham and speeding along the dip to Great Missenden before haring down Wendover Bank to Aylesbury. If they were in good mechanical order and with good quality coal, those 5MTs dealt dismissively with the lightweight four-vehicle trains, the results making a visit over the doomed line even more attractive. It was very wise not to 'window hang' because an eyeful of smut and cinders would necessitate a visit to the pharmacy for some eye solution the following day.

If on the 14.38 Nottingham Victoria departure, it was essential to look out when passing Neasden to see the 16.38 ex-Marylebone locomotive, which had arrived on the returning newspaper empties from Nottingham. If she was 'required', I would alight at Aylesbury and backtrack on a DMU to Harrow-on-the-Hill to travel on the latter train as far as either Aylesbury or Woodford Halse. If she wasn't, I would continue north, where on Saturdays Excepted (SX) days a 17.20 starting train from Rugby Central would be standing in the down loop. If that was a 'requirement', I would alight there and catch it to the lonely outpost of Ashby Magna, not being able to make Leicester Central for the final southbound train of the day (the 17.15 Nottingham Victoria to Marylebone) because of the notoriously bad timekeeping.

I sometimes wondered, during the forty minutes I had at Leicester Central when all the above variations failed to produce any 'requirements', what would I have looked like when accompanying my father on our visits to our relations each December, loaded with Christmas gifts. Short trousers, short back and sides haircut maybe? More annoying was that, understandably, my father never recorded which locomotives had taken us there on our Sunday excursions. V2s or A3s? I will never know. When the line was demoted and the Sunday services curtailed, we travelled out of St Pancras with unrecorded Jubilees and Scots!

With my newly acquired wealth from promotion within the clerical ranks, I purchased a privilege season ticket to Basingstoke (at 10*s* per week, mind!) and my outings increasing significantly. Tuesday, 15 February saw *Tamar Valley* red-lined; I caught her on the 17.30 out of Waterloo. This was a crowded commuter train, and I often chose to stand all the way, observing the mileposts to record the speeds and the train's progress. This was far preferable to receiving tut-tutting from the bowler-hat brigade from behind their evening papers when attempting to do the same from a seat in an open vestibule. Although following prolonged speeds in the mid-70s and passing Woking in under twenty-seven minutes, delays over the single-line section between Hook and Basingstoke (only the down local was in use, due to engineering work in connection with the electrification) resulted in an on-time arrival at Basingstoke of 18.33.

A double Woking trip on 23 February was well worth the effort with two more West Countries being red-lined. They were *Ilfracombe* on the 18.39 arrival and *Dartmoor* on the 20.25 arrival – the latter maxing at 80mph approaching Hampton Court Junction. The following evening, with the temperature dropping to a low of 2°C, 34071 *601 Squadron* stopped at Woking, the West Byfleet signalman having noted no lights on the Bulleid. It was apparently an electrical fault and replacement oil lamps were eventually found. This conveniently allowed me to alight for a 'required' Standard 5MT working the following 17.43 Basingstoke stopper.

Tuesday, 15 February and the down 'Bournemouth Belle' is gathering speed past Wimbledon 'B' signalbox with Light Pacific 34087 *145 Squadron* in charge.

Mondays excepted, the 08.16 Kensington (Olympia) departed from Clapham Junction's Platform 17 each day. On Wednesday, 16 February, Standard 3MT 82019 was the power – a locomotive with which I accrued over 100 miles during 1967, making seventeen return trips en route from my Kent home to my workplace at Wimbledon.

The final outing that month was an overnight to the Somerset & Dorset (S&D), with the bus company supplying replacement road transport, thus allowing the delayed closure of the line to proceed, having finally got their act together. This scenic line, which was opened throughout in 1863, was principally constructed in the hope of luring freight from the Bristol Channel to the south coast which would otherwise travel by sea around the coast of Cornwall. In addition, following successful promotion by the London, Midland & Scottish (LMS) of through-trains from the Midlands to Bournemouth, the line was stretched to its limit to cope with the resultant traffic, albeit predominantly on summer Saturdays. With the motor car and foreign holidays being enjoyed by the populace in the late 1950s and early 1960s, the line was left to meagre local traffic. A deliberate diversion via Reading of the 'Pines Express' in 1962 saw the final nail in the coffin, thus the line qualified for inclusion within the Beeching Report as a loss-making line.

My final visit to the S&D was on Saturday, 26 February – a week before its delayed closure was enacted. Eulogised in Flanders & Swann's 'Slow Train', my thoughts were with the Midsomer Norton signalman who was possibly contemplating redundancy or a move to a power box. Since 1995, a preservation group has taken over the site and operates trains over a small section of track.

Bournemouth's 76011 has her tanks replenished at Evercreech Junction while working that day's 06.00 Bristol Temple Meads to Branksome train.

Following our visit to the S&D we went westwards to Wareham, where one of 70F's Mickey Tanks, Ivatt 41320, was caught working an 11.28 departure for Swanage. With services over the branch being turned over to DEMUs that September, Bournemouth's stud of tank locomotives was slimmed down; this 2-6-2T, however, survived until the end of SR steam in July 1967.

Rather than getting DL mileage on an overnight train from Paddington to Bristol, my lifelong friend Alan and I travelled out of Waterloo on the 22.35 Travelling Post Office (TPO) Weymouth departure, alighting at Eastleigh for the 02.02 Hymeck DL-powered Bristol via Salisbury service. It was my fourth visit to this iconic line. Our train, the 06.00 Bristol Temple Meads to Branksome, the SR authorities not being disposed to allow these insignificant trains into Bournemouth Central and the West having closed the previous year, was powered to the subsequent preserved station of Bath Green Park by a Warship DL. The stop-gap timetable was, in my opinion, deliberately designed to deter any prospective customers. An example being the train we were on, which was taking four and a half hours to travel the 82¼ miles – thus allowing sufficient time at Bath to bunk the shed in the pre-dawn darkness.

Although the WR had retained thirteen tank locomotives, whether they were all operational was a moot point and the power over the Mendips that morning was an externally filthy Bournemouth-allocated BR Mogul. It was very cold, and a fresh layer of snow cosseted the dimly lit passenger-less stations on the route. It was sad to witness the managed decline by the authorities – a week later the line was history.

Upon reaching the still-vibrant steam scenario at Poole, our demeanour improved. After a brief visit to the Swanage branch, Alan made his way home to the Smoke while I enjoyed some new steam track on the once-a-day Plymouth to Brighton train – on this occasion worked, from Salisbury, by Light Pacific *Ilfracombe*.

MARCH MADNESS
SHREWSBURY, EXETER & CARLISLE

On four occasions in March I was to be found on the 17.36 Kensington (Olympia) to Clapham Junction, en route to the Rules & Signalling evening class. These were very crowded trains, and I would often have to sit knee to knee (six a side) with others in a compartment in the leading futuristic fibre-glass vehicle – there was no room to document speeds or write in my notebook. It was the *only* method of catching runs with Nine Elms tanks.

Of those four occasions, just two were red-lined: 80133 and 80143. The first had arrived from Landore to the SR at Feltham in the August of 1964 and the second had arrived at Feltham from Brighton in July 1963. Both transferred to Nine Elms in November 1964.

Wednesday, 2 March saw me collect a run with *213 Squadron* on the 17.09. I wrote in my notebook that not only was she my last 'required' Modified Pacific but also my last Battle of Britain. As an aside, in my naivety, I initially thought there were two separate classes of Bulleid Light Pacifics. I was unaware that there was no difference, other than the naming, between the West Country and Battle of Britain locomotives. Offering further confusion, to my mind, were the differing examples of the Modified (Rebuilt) and Unmodified with their shiny (when clean), streamlined casing. This is the first occasion I have admitted my misunderstanding – at least in print!

In the meantime, it was deemed necessary by the managers of my new clerical position at the South Eastern HQ near Cannon Street that I was required to have an understanding of the geography of Kent, i.e., sidings, junctions, etc.

Thursday, 3 March saw me enjoying a day out in connection with my recent promotion within the BR clerical grades to a position within the South Eastern (SR) Division. As I was conveniently armed with a camera, here ex-SECR C 0-6-0 DS239 (formerly 31592) was photographed at Ashford Works. Its withdrawal the following year led to a lifetime of preservation at the Bluebell Railway.

A refugee from Southampton Docks, DS237 *Maunsell* (formerly 30065) has also had a fortunate life, being taken into preservation at the Kent & East Sussex Railway (K&ESR).

And finally, yet another USA 0-6-0T, DS238 *Wainwright* (formerly 30070), a transfer from Southampton Docks, attempts to hide behind some axles outside the main Ashford Works. Fortune shone upon these two USA tanks. En route from Ashford Works to Dai Woodham's scrap yard in South Wales, they suffered a hot box and were put away in Tonbridge West Yard. During the time spent there they were both purchased by the K&ESR organisation for a lifetime in preservation.

I can assure readers that the Stanier 5MT depicted here, departing Aylesbury in the gathering gloom on Saturday, 5 March with the 16.38 Marylebone to Nottingham Victoria, is Colwick-allocated 45267. Having caught her sister 16B-allocated 45324 out of Marylebone on the earlier 14.38 departure, I had doubled back from Aylesbury to Harrow-on-the-Hill for this capture. What then, you may ask? A very lengthy near two-hour wait in an unheated waiting room for the 45333-worked 17.15 Nottingham Victoria to Marylebone – dedication or what?

To that end, in early March, accompanied by an inspector who was well versed in rules and signalling, a tour of Kent was undertaken, fortuitously calling in at Ashford Works with camera in hand.

Two Saturday visits to the ex-GC line out of Marylebone that month yielded six Colwick-allocated Blackies. On 5 March, 45267 rewarded me with a fantastic 86mph down Wendover Bank, and on 19th, at a more moderate pace, the returning 17.15 ex-Nottingham had a Gresley non-corridor vehicle at its rear in which I bounced and swung along the 38 miles from Aylesbury. The dedication to the meagre diet of trains over this line was surely tested back then. The cold, unheated waiting room at Aylesbury was not necessarily conducive to one's perseverance – with no internet or even Walkman to while away the two hours.

Sunday, 6 March was the final day of the Adur Valley line, with services from Brighton to Horsham via Steyning ceasing at close of service that day. Opened in 1861 by the London, Brighton & South Coast Railway, it was, unusually for a branch line, double-tracked throughout its 20-mile length.

Two weeks later and having earlier travelled to Southampton and back, I crossed London to collect runs with three more Colwick-allocated Black 5MTs. Adopting the same plan here, at Aylesbury in slightly improved lighting, 28-year-old 45464 is waiting for the off with the 16.38 Marylebone to Nottingham Victoria.

This was in anticipation of the never-realised through traffic from the L&SWR at Guildford with the line subsequently relying on income from rural and agricultural means.

The method Beeching used to calculate whether a line was paying its way was through the revenue from sales of tickets at the stations on the route. In this case, as they were frequented predominantly by users coming into the line from elsewhere (for example, walkers and ramblers), the financial figures were skewed against the line. Fortunately, I had already travelled over the line by steam with one of Brighton's Mickey tanks in the summer of 1963.

Rather than going direct from London, a group of us travelled with WC *Holsworthy* out of Waterloo on the 10.30 Weymouth departure to Southampton. Due to engineering works in connection with the Bournemouth line electrification, this train was diverted via the Guildford New Line (Effingham Junction), the Pompey Direct and Fareham, causing a fair amount of head turning, waving and photographing by those witnessing it en route. We then made our way to Shoreham-by-Sea, and as the DEMU progressed towards Horsham, at the staffed stations, train doors were held open while others dashed to the booking office for souvenir tickets, some of which were of Southern Railway antiquity and dated that final day.

The following week – with John Lennon having caused national outrage with his remark about being more popular than Jesus and *The Frost Report* launching the careers of John Cleese, Ronnie Barker and Ronnie Corbett – saw me making the most of my newly acquired season ticket. I was now to be found most evenings heading out to Basingstoke – 34015 *Exmouth* and 73043 and 35008 *Orient Line*, with 73018 and 73088 all being red-lined.

On Saturday, 12 March, a Footex was run from Southampton to Wolverhampton. Initially diagrammed for *Clan Line*, she had failed earlier in the week and a filthy *Port Line* stood in. For reasons not documented, we were thirty-four minutes late into Wolverhampton. While the fans went to the match, a group of six of us travelled north on a Paddington to Birkenhead Woodside train, which was steam-hauled north of Shrewsbury and just managed to squeeze in two runs of 18 miles each way to and from Gobowen. On arrival there, and having raced over the footbridge to the waiting southbound train, we were then treated to a heart-stopping eighteen minutes and two seconds run, with 84mph being attained between Baschurch and Leaton. Upon our return to Wolverhampton, the enthusiast grapevine had been activated and a further two dozen of our Brummie colleagues joined us. The day was

Diverted via the Pompey Direct due to engineering work in connection with the Bournemouth electrification, Battle of Britain 34056 *Croydon* is seen arriving at Havant on Sunday, 6 March with the 12.30 'Bournemouth Belle' Waterloo to Bournemouth Central. A Salisbury-allocated Pacific, and having been displaced from Exmouth Junction in 1963, she, along with other 70E Bulleids, was always kept in excellent external condition. Unlike other SR sheds, there was no shortage of cleaners there.

That same day was the Adur Valley line's last day of existence and it closed between Shoreham-by-Sea and Horsham just hours later. While this station, Southwater, was demolished to make way for road improvements, a fair section of the former track bed is now part of the Downs Link footpath.

rounded off quite nicely with a 'required' Standard Mogul on the evening Weymouth to Woking all-stations stopper.

On 15 March, the locomotive that was to become my favourite (everyone has one, don't they?), Battle of Britain 34052 *Lord Dowding*, attained 85mph along the racing stretch between Fleet and Farnborough with the lightweight 18.35 ex-Salisbury.

A twelve-locomotive Southern Region outing was undertaken on 25 and 26 March, starting with a 'required' 73088 *Joyous Gard* on the 17.09 out of Waterloo. After returning to London, I then headed as far west as I could without being stranded for the night on the 21.20 Waterloo to Brockenhurst. This station was opened in 1847 on completion of the Southampton and Dorchester Railway, which made its way over the somewhat circuitous Castleman's Corkscrew via Wimborne. A more direct cut-off via Christchurch to Bournemouth was opened in 1888.

Anyway, back to this night and this move, made to attain the maximum amount of sleep overnight, was to be replicated on many more occasions over

With the locomotive number 45311 just about discernible through the smoke and grime at Gobowen on Saturday, 12 March, this Shrewsbury-allocated Black 5MT is waiting for the crossing gates to open while working that day's 12.10 Paddington to Birkenhead Woodside. Looks are deceptive – she had just attained a maximum of 75mph.

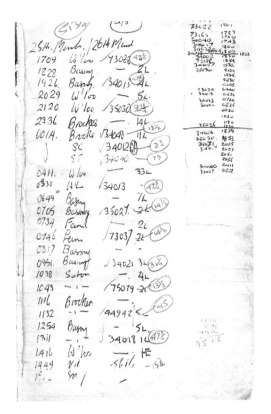

A notebook extract depicting my SR overnight bash on Friday and Saturday, 25–26 March.

the coming months. Arriving at Brockenhurst at 23.36, the 'bed' for the night, in the form of the 22.13 TPO Weymouth to Waterloo, arrived shortly after midnight and then took four hours for the 95 miles to Waterloo (there were lengthy station stops for the then extensive mail and parcel traffic).

Conveying just one or two passenger vehicles, it was an ideal scenario to get some shuteye. The warm compartment, in which shoes were taken off, blinds pulled down and lights dimmed, was heaven to a chaser in readiness for a lengthy day's bashing over the following twelve hours or so. On this occasion, unlike several others later in the year, I didn't have to worry about missing the 03.00 Woking stop. I slept soundly into Waterloo, arriving there thirty-three minutes late at 04.44, apparently the result of engineering works in the Winchester area.

Before its closure that September, the train called in and reversed at Southampton terminus station – a somewhat unusual locomotive diagramming move, which was noted at the time. The train locomotive, 34040 *Crewkerne*, which had worked the TPO into Southampton Central, was detached and disappeared into the tunnel. A tender-first sister took the train around to the Terminus Station only for *Crewkerne* to reappear, having reversed at Northam Junction to take the train forward to London. The remainder of that Saturday, although I was hopping on and off trains throughout Hampshire, yielded just one 'required' catch: Banbury's 44942 on the Poole to York service.

The following day, 345 miles of A4 haulage was enjoyed aboard the Locomotive Club of Great Britain (LCGB)-organised 'A4 Commemorative Tour' to Exeter and back, costing nearly a week's wages at 63s. Aberdeen-allocated 60024 *Kingfisher* was the selected locomotive and some fine running was recorded with many instances of 80mph-plus.

It wasn't looking too healthy for steam fans in the north-west of England with the news that from the summer timetable, commencing two weeks hence, all trains between Euston and Crewe would be worked by electric locomotives (ELs). By default, this meant that the resulting displacement of DLs, predominantly English Electric (EE) Type 4s, would be cascaded to work services, currently steam-powered north of Crewe. I therefore spent many hours studying the LMR timetable, resulting in a four-night, 1,443-mile jaunt. Thrown into the mix was the cessation of the overnight sleeper trains to Windermere and Whitehaven – the first being completely withdrawn and the latter being terminated at Barrow with the sleepers themselves being detached at Preston.

Previous overnight journeys to the west of England, Newcastle and Scotland had involved through-trains, enabling me to enjoy warm, comfortable accommodation throughout the night. Excepting the initial journey to the Cumbrian town of Whitehaven, this proposed itinerary involved many hours on station platforms and in waiting rooms to while away the time between trains during the lengthy night hours. Although it briefly crossed my mind whether I had the stamina and staying-awake powers to encompass such an outing, the adrenalin pumping through my veins at the thought of the many new locations and classes of steam locomotives I might witness overrode any negative worries. My parents also never expressed any concerns – they were grateful that I had chosen the risk-free hobby of trainspotting rather than any more hazardous alternatives.

So, with Harold Wilson's government en route to securing a landslide majority of ninety-six seats in progress (Labour was down to a single-seat majority a month previously) and having negotiated my way through the demolition site allegedly called Euston Station, which was being rebuilt in connection with the West Coast Main Line (WCML) electrification, I caught the 23.15 departure for Whitehaven. The forecast was ominous, with snow-laden clouds threatening to deposit their contents upon dawn breaking, while skirting the Cumbrian coast: The Walker Brothers' 'The Sun Ain't Gonna Shine Anymore' was somewhat prophetic.

Promotion meant more money. More money meant I could afford to travel on rail tours. Here, I'm on my first, on Sunday, 27 March. Visiting A4 60024 *Kingfisher* rests at Exeter St David's on a 345-mile outing from London. Four months later, I was to catch a run with her on 'The Granite Express' between Aberdeen and Glasgow prior to her withdrawal that September.

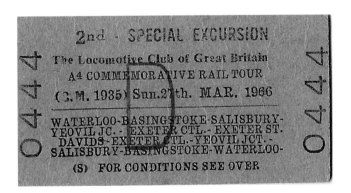

The accompanying ticket.

Arriving a mere five minutes late, I made my way the short distance to Workington. Those 7 miles of this former Furness Railway line, which was finally completed in 1850, were in fact the most problematic to construct, running alongside the Irish Sea on a ledge hewn from the cliffs. After having bunked the shed at Workington, I observed a closure notice for the line from there to Penrith via Cockermouth, so a hastily amended train plan was undertaken to encompass the line.

This wonderfully scenic railway opened in 1865, despite strong objections by the local poet William Wordsworth stating that it encroached on 'his terrain'. It had Cockermouth as one of its stations – immortalised in the 1964 song by Flanders & Swann, 'Slow Train'. Even the truncated stub off the WCML at Penrith to Keswick succumbed to closure, albeit later in 1972.

During the five hours I had at Carlisle, I visited both Kingmoor and Upperby sheds, following directions as shown in 'the bunker's bible', Aidan L.F. Fuller's *Locoshed Directory*. Although it contained warnings against trespassing in motive power depots without the necessary authentication documents, I personally never bothered with such detail – if challenged, on producing my BR identity card the usual comment was 'I haven't seen you', thus exonerating the foreman should any mishap befall me.

Captured in the passing loop opposite Workington Shed, Kingmoor-allocated 44982 awaits signals with a northbound freight on Thursday, 31 March.

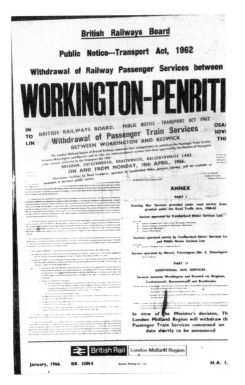

The closure notice on Workington Station, which prompted an immediate revision of my plans to travel over this most scenic of lines.

The instructions on how to get to Kingmoor and Upperby sheds at Carlisle, as detailed in Fuller's *British Locomotive Shed Directory*.

12A CARLISLE (KINGMOOR)

The shed is on the east side of the main line about 1½ miles north of Carlisle Station. The yard is visible from the line.

Leave Carlisle Station by the main entrance and go straight ahead into Court Square. Turn left along English Street and continue into Scotch Street and Rickergate. Cross Eden Bridge and continue up Stanwix Bank. Turn left at the top of Etterby Street and continue along Etterby Scaur. Turn left at the top of the hill into Etterby Road. A broad cinder path leads to the shed from the right-hand side of this road (just before the railway bridge). Walking time 45 minutes. A bus service (C3 or C4 St. Anns) runs from English Street to the end of Etterby Road (200 yards from the shed entrance).

Diesel stabling point: **CARLISLE NEW YARD.**

12B CARLISLE (UPPERBY)

The shed is on the east side of the main Penrith line south of Carlisle Station. The yard is visible from the line.

Leave Carlisle Station by the main entrance and go straight ahead into Court Square. Turn right into Botchergate and continue into London Road. Turn right into Tyne Street (just past the railway underbridge). This is a short cul-de-sac, and a cinder path leads to the shed from a gate at the end. Walking time 20 minutes.

23

Motive power depots back then were wonderful cathedrals of steam – the sepulchral gloom, the filth, oil, ash, pits, coal, the intoxicating aroma, the potential for accidents when failing to notice abandoned equipment laid out for the unwary and water spilled out of hoses and frozen into dangerous puddles. Although many organisations arranged coach trips specially to 'bash sheds', I only visited them if my schedule allowed the time.

At Kingmoor, examples of 'Flying Pigs', Stanier 5MT and 8Fs, Brits and 9Fs totalling twenty-four were in steam. On the condemned siding were Patriot *Sir Frank Ree* and Scot *Scots Guardsman*, while at Upperby, a far cleaner round-house-equipped shed, twenty-one locomotives were in steam, comprising of Mickey tanks, Black 5s, Ivatt 3MTs and Brits.

The reason I had scheduled an extended period of time at Carlisle was that the only steam-worked train (that I was aware of) to Bradford via Ais Gill was the 16.37 all-stations stopper. The weather was worsening and the higher we went the more snow was encountered. With the steam heating leaking from the ageing LMS set of coaches, along with calling at the passengerless gaslit stations, I really thought the scene was set for becoming stranded in the middle of nowhere. When the welcome lights of Skipton hove into view I breathed a sigh of relief.

Roger Price, a fellow enthusiast, had written to all the regions asking which passenger trains remained steam operated. With the typewritten resulting booklet (all proceeds to the Woking Homes orphanage) clutched in my hand, I made my way via Leeds, witnessing the mind-blowing scene of the many steelworks furnaces illuminating the darkness, to Sheffield to catch the 02.00 Leeds departure, which was allegedly rostered for a Holbeck 5MT.

PASTURES NEW
WINDERMERE, MANCHESTER & LONGMOOR

Sure enough, Roger's publication turned up trumps. Holbeck-allocated 45204 took me the 39½ miles to the draughty, windswept 'tunnel' of Leeds City Station. The purpose of this train, to this day, baffles me – five or six BR Mark 1, fluorescent-lit, open saloon vehicles with no parcels or mail usage. An otherwise empty stock move, perhaps?

After finishing off some partially crushed sandwiches and suffering a Peak DL over to Bradford following two runs with Manningham's Fairburn tanks, I headed to Harrogate for the only steam-powered departure in Roger's book – the 11.40 for King's Cross. This was a four-vehicle portion worked to Leeds Central by B1 61199.

The Leeds/Bradford to Morecambe services via the 'Little North Western' were to be turned over to DMUs at the April timetable change, so the remainder of the day was spent station-hopping on them. Gracing Skipton's and Hellifield's platforms with my presence, I collected runs with several Black 5s, with Brit *Clive of India* in the mix. I then headed south on a disappointingly DL-hauled train to the axis station of Crewe.

What would us gricers have done back then without the warmth and sustenance provision of the all-night open refreshment room at Crewe? With most meals accompanied with chips and tea, one could secrete oneself in a corner for some shuteye while waiting for the next train.

Following a change of trains at the freezing Wigan North Western platform, I departed there on the 03.23 Brit 28 *Royal Star*-hauled Windermere sleeper service. Sleep deprivation must have finally caught up with me because the next thing I know was being shaken awake having arrived at the lakeside terminus. The weather had deteriorated considerably with heavy snow causing the train to amass a 100-minute-late arrival at 07.33.

Opened from the West Coast Main Line (WCML) station at Oxenholme in 1847, despite once again being objected to by the local poet William Wordsworth (surely, in today's terminology, a 'nimby'), the terminus was equipped with an overall trainshed roof and four platforms. Although still extant on my visit, this was reduced to a single-platform, one-train line in 1973 and further truncated twelve years later – the main station buildings were sold to a supermarket.

After visiting the turntable, *Royal Star* returned me to Preston, and I was now fully awake to witness the glorious snow-covered Lancashire vista en route. During the very cold remaining daylight hours that Saturday, I tootled up and down the WCML on trains destined to either cease altogether or be turned over to DL haulage with the imminent timetable change. It was in times like those, waiting on freezing platforms for late-running trains, that I questioned my sanity. But then again, it was all disappearing – it had to be done.

The notebook extract of my 30 March–3 April travels.

Making my way to Manchester, I headed for my overnight bed's home to the Smoke, the 22.50 Manchester Central to Marylebone. This was the second of six occasions when I caught this GC line-routed train and not once were there any other enthusiasts aboard. Indeed, after departure from Sheffield Victoria nor were there any 'normal' passengers – just as well, as the formation was just two LMS vehicles and one van.

The 216-mile, six-and-a-quarter-hour journey had an unbelievable five traction changes! A Trafford Park steam locomotive took the train on a circuitous trip around the Mancunian suburbs via the wonderfully named Throstle Nest Junction to Guide Bridge, handing over there to a direct current (DC) EL for the Woodhead route to Sheffield. There, a Brush-type DL (Type 3 or 4) took us the 65 miles to Leicester Central where, at 02.45, a tender-first Black 5MT, which was en route home to Banbury Shed (having been working north out of Marylebone the previous evening), took us the 34 miles to Woodford Halse where the final leg into London was worked by a Sulzer Type 2 'Splutterbug' DL.

Although a section of the line north of Leicester was to remain open as a preserved line and certain parts would become the template for the track-bed for HS2, the majority would return to nature – as it was before 1899 when the route was constructed – or be built upon. It was paramount for the history books that accurate documentation was made, and to this end, it was important for me to stay awake to record the number of the steam locomotive taking over the train at Leicester – only once did I rely on the accuracy of the guard's journal on reaching London.

Arriving into Marylebone just after 05.00 usually led me to take a pleasant walk via Park Lane to Victoria for the first train to my Kent home. On this occasion, however, after feasting on a fry-up at a café near Waterloo, a further 245 steam miles aboard the SR Mogul and Q1-powered 'Wilts & Hants Rail Tour' was undertaken – the latter allegedly having been withdrawn some months previously.

I made two further trips out of Marylebone that month, both with Annesley's 45190 on the 14.38 departure. The first was a Maundy Thursday when the train was strengthened to four vehicles, perhaps in the hope of an increase in passengers. With just one occupant per compartment, was it worth it? In reality, most prospective customers had already assumed the line had ceased and probably either went by road or the alternative Midland Line out of St Pancras.

The photographic stop at Mortimer on Sunday, 3 April, sees Moguls U 31639 and N 31411 pause while working the 'Wilts & Hants Rail Tour'.

Upon arrival into Salisbury both Moguls were serviced on 70E, N 31411 having just three weeks remaining before her withdrawal from her home shed of Guildford.

With, by that date, no booked passenger work for Salisbury's stud of Standard Moguls, unless they were utilised by the shed foreman when visiting other depots, they were a nightmare to obtain haulage with. Fortunately, this one – 76067 resting deep inside 70E – was caught just three weeks prior to the end of SR steam when working the 16.46 Weymouth to Bournemouth Central.

BR Standard 2-6-0 76007 is dead inside Salisbury Shed. In a similar scenario to the previous shot, I was to catch her working the 18.51 Bournemouth Central to Woking just twelve days before the end of SR steam in July 1967.

Although officially withdrawn earlier that year, together with the remaining examples of her class, Bulleid Q1 0-6-0 33006 was specifically kept for this rail tour and is seen at Salisbury awaiting departure for Waterloo.

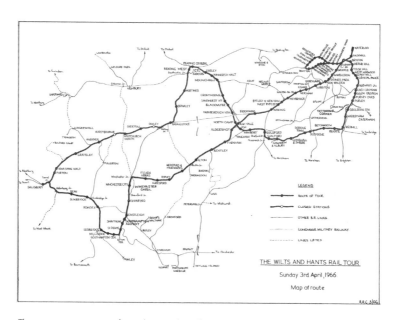

The route map extract from the tour brochure.

On 18 April there was a 'required' 44835 on the 17.20 Rugby starter. This meant alighting at Ashby Magna, as I couldn't make Leicester Central without missing the last remaining London-bound train home. I was usually the only passenger alighting there and was viewed with suspicion (when the station was manned!) as I didn't leave the station, often taking refuge in the gents' toilet to avoid any ticket checks. All was worth it, with Stanier 5MT 45288, my fifth Colwick-allocated locomotive scratched that month, taking me back to the Smoke.

On Saturday, 9 April, a further two Banbury-allocated Black 5s were caught on the Poole to York service and the return trains while I was on a Hampshire bash, with *Clan Line* and Standard Mogul 76053 in the mix.

On the following Tuesday, the Salisbury foreman must have been short of a fit locomotive for the 18.35 Waterloo train because he turned round the now preserved Standard 4MT 75069 in forty minutes. She had arrived there on the 16.51 stopper from Basingstoke.

45190 waits patiently for the off at Marylebone with the 14.38 for Nottingham Victoria on 7 April. Transferred from Annesley at that shed's closure to steam three months earlier, there must have been a shortage of smokebox shedplates at her new depot of Colwick. As it was Maundy Thursday, the train had been strengthened to four vehicles, causing replatforming from 4 to 3. She was to survive into 1968 and was withdrawn from Heaton Mersey that May.

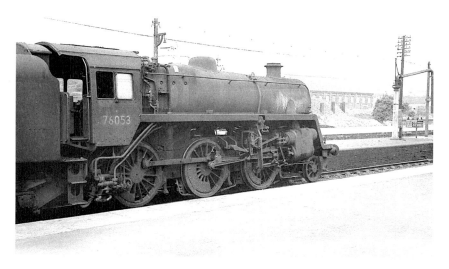

Having caught a run with 11-year-old BR Mogul 76053 in April, here she is at Basingstoke eight weeks later on engineering duties. This nomadic Standard had been allocated to Redhill, Salisbury, Guildford and Feltham prior to her present one at Eastleigh.

Saturday, 16 April, and a run-past featuring 0-6-0ST WD196 *Errol Lonsdale* was organised over the Hollywater Loop, a 6-mile circular route within Longmoor Camp on which the Royal Electrical and Mechanical Engineers (REME) (army) practised every kind of engineering skill. The locomotive has survived into preservation in Belgium.

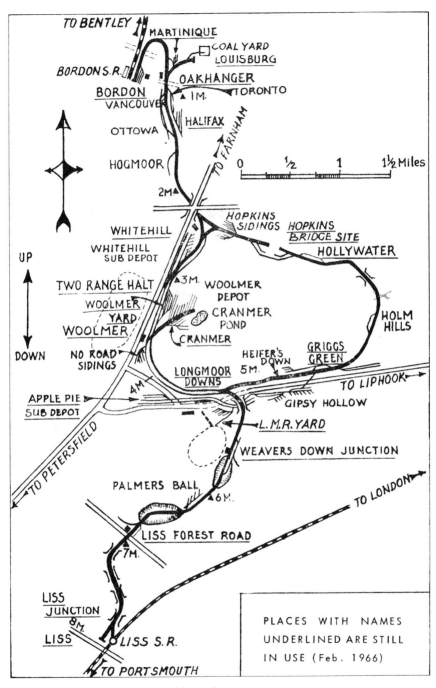

The map extract from the brochure of the Hollywater Loop.

The first 'Longmoor Rail Tour' was embarked upon on 16 April (due to high demand, a second was run on 30th) with the now preserved 2-10-0 WD600 *Gordon* working it from Woking to Staines via Liss and Borden. Initially opened as a tramway between Longmoor and Borden and called the Woolmer Instructional Military Railway, it was converted to standard gauge between the years 1905 and 1907. Following an extension to Liss in 1933, it attained the name Longmoor Military Railway two years later. With its military usage declining, the site was vacated in 1969. Sadly, a preservation group failed in its attempt to save it due to local residents' objections.

Personally, the catch of the day was Standard 3MT 77014, which took the train down the Windsor branch. With most of my colleagues having secured a run with her as a pilot, on a diverted Sunday train over 'The Alps', she was wonderfully red-lined in my Ian Allan *Locoshed* book. I believe the original plan was to send the SR more displaced examples of this class but, with the end of steam becoming ever closer, the scheme was abandoned.

The following Tuesday, having attended a meeting at Chatham for work, I got away early enough for a midweek Bournemouth outing and luck was with me as the 'required' Merchant 13 *Blue Funnel* was on the 15.30 Weymouth departure – maxing at 82½mph down Winchester Bank. I returned to London that evening on the 18.35 departure from Bournemouth – a train designated by us enthusiasts as the 'club' train because whatever any of us were doing or chasing, we nearly always ended up on this 20.51 arrival into Waterloo. The restaurant/buffet portion was added on at Bournemouth and although I forget the precise shunting arrangements for the attachment on the rear of the Weymouth train, my notes from the day indicate I obtained a shunt movement with 70F Mickey 41316 – yes, all movements count for a red-line entry. I was living the dream with 216 Merchant steam miles after work!

The following night saw Unmodified Light Pacific 34006 *Bude* on the light-weight Salisbury run. What can only be described as a massive jolt occurred (almost throwing me across to the opposite seat) whilst at mid-60mph near Fleet. Apparently, the 'Unrebuilds' are prone to their ratcheted reversing lever coming loose and occasionally slipping out – on this evening, the fireman was having to maintain it in a forward position as well as feeding the fire!

Another Saturday, and another visit to Hampshire (times three!) was made on 23 April, with 415 miles of steam mileage being accrued. Starting out on the *25 Squadron*-hauled 08.35 ex-Waterloo, twenty-three minutes were lost en route to Southampton due to 'brake trouble'. With just twelve minutes on

Southampton Central's platforms, I was heading back to London on the 13.03 arrival, *Aberdeen Commonwealth*, making a mockery of the timings, without exceeding 75mph, by clipping thirteen minutes off the schedule with her ten-vehicle train.

After I grabbed a sandwich, her sister Merchant, *Blue Star*, returned me to Basingstoke on the 13.30 Weymouth train, where, in the lengthiest wait of the day, an hour was endured before the Giesl Ejector-equipped Flat, *Fighter Command*, deposited me into Waterloo just after 16.00. I then took 'The Royal Wessex' 16.35 train back down to Southampton Nederland Line, maxing at a modest 77mph down Winchester Bank.

I popped down to Redbridge on a Hymek DL-worked local in an unsuccessful bid for a catch on the 17.42 Bournemouth Central to Eastleigh stopper. As mentioned earlier, all-day visits to the area always culminated – together with several other like-minded chasers – on the 'Club Train', the 20.51 arrival into Waterloo, on this occasion worked by the subsequently preserved *Clan Line*.

A resplendent Battle of Britain 34052 *Lord Dowding* is at Basingstoke having arrived with the 17.09 from Waterloo on Friday, 29 April. She was to become a firm favourite of mine. So much so that when passing her sitting in the bay at Basingstoke waiting to work the 19.06 Eastleigh departure on the final Friday of SR steam, while I was aboard the 17.23 Waterloo to Bournemouth Central, I alighted at Winchester to catch my final 7 miles of haulage on her last passenger train.

What a wonderful way to spend a Saturday – it wasn't to last, so the most was made of my season ticket.

The 17.30 ex-Waterloo had a late start on the 27th with the inward 16.51 arrival having been delayed due to 'operational difficulties' – in fact, an additional stop was made in the Winchester area to collect parcels and mail that had been strewn out of a preceding parcel train with its doors open.

On the final Saturday that month, having arrived into Waterloo from Southampton on the 13.03 arrival, I had planned to cross London for a trip down the GC. With a pristine 34019 *Bideford* on the 13.30 departure, however, I changed my mind and travelled with her to Brockenhurst. Why alight there, one might ask?

Always on the lookout for a 'required' Bournemouth-allocated tank on the Lymington branch, 80094 sated that need with the bonus of her sister, 80083, taking me back to Southampton to connect into the *Honiton*-worked 'club train'. For the football followers among you, Liverpool won the First Division that day for the second time in three seasons.

Eastleigh's Unmodified Pacific 34019 *Bideford* is at Waterloo with the 13.30 Weymouth departure on Saturday, 30 April. Having already been to Southampton and back earlier that day, I was intending to cross London for Black 5 haulage out of Marylebone. However, with the increasing rate of withdrawal of Bulleid's 'Spam Cans', I was minded for a 92-mile trip to Brockenhurst with her.

MAY

TANGERINE TRAVELS
YORKSHIRE, LEICESTER & BIRKENHEAD

The 17.36 ex-Kensington (Olympia) was caught on the first two Tuesdays that May, Standard tanks 82019 and 80145 being red-lined. It was as if I was swimming against the tide of withdrawals. Would I get all of 70A tanks before the cutter's torch? As mentioned within the Introduction, I naively dismissed the Rules & Signalling classes as a bore so, although still arriving at Clapham Junction at 17.44 off the Post Office train, I then headed to Waterloo for a journey out on the 18.00 Salisbury train. By now, I wasn't so bothered about hunting down the few remaining Pacifics that I 'required' haulage with – they would appear in due course, providing the grim reaper hadn't already taken them. I was more interested in mileage accumulation before steam finished.

Unlike the other rush-hour stoppers formed on Mark 1 stock, the 18.00 departure was usually formed of Bulleid open coaches with wide windows and comfortable seats and was never overcrowded. With bowler-hatted city gents reading their evening newspapers and smoking their pipes, it was a very genteel commute; nothing like today's mobile phone users informing all of their dreary existence or music heard from ill-fitting earphones. My evening 'commute' to Basingstoke was gathering pace and, although nothing spectacular was noted, I was relishing the sunsets – the month being particularly pleasant weather wise – and accumulating mileages behind traction that was destined to disappear the following year. This, of course, running together with a daily record of which locomotives were in circulation, which adorned my tattered notebooks.

Away from railways, The Beatles performed their final British concert at Wembley, while Swinging Radio England, playing Manfred Mann's 'Pretty Flamingo', commenced broadcasting off the south coast of England and the Moors Murderers were sentenced to life imprisonment.

Saturday, 7 May saw my first of two visits to the GC that month. Passengers were few and far between. Although service withdrawal notices had just been posted on the Aylesbury to Rugby and north of Nottingham sections, most customers had already deserted the dying line, with the regular disruptive loco-motive failures not assisting matters. As if to quantify that, on Friday, 27 May, a fifty-three-minute delay while locomotives were exchanged at Culworth Junction was endured on the returning 17.15 ex-Nottingham; this was not appreciated by me as none of my 'required' locomotives were involved.

With my appetite whetted by last month's visit to the North Eastern Region (NER), in the early hours of Friday 13th I was to be seen once again aboard the 02.00 Sheffield Midland to Leeds City. Plagued by traction changes that had been made in the summer timetable (with tangerine-coloured covers) last month (which my travelling companion Paul and I were unaware of), several abortive steamless hours were spent idling time away at York, although a compensa-tory shed bash to 50A was savoured. Having misread the timetable, we then became stranded at Wakefield's somewhat derelict Kirkgate Station, the time fortunately passing by with a seemingly continuous parade of War Department (WD)-hauled freight trains.

Matters improved by late afternoon with a visit to Doncaster and several catches on the Bradford portions out of both Exchange and Forster Square stations. Oh, how I loved those portions! On the Bradford Exchange ones, the Low Moor or Wakefield foreman would turn out anything from five dif-ferent steam classes – the named B1s being especially appreciated. Once, these locomotives worked prestige expresses throughout the country but the few remaining, and I have to say, not in the best of condition, were destined to eke out their lives on these 17-mile, three-vehicle trains.

The overnight 'beds' on that night were courtesy of the Aberystwyth TPO, which deposited us at York at 03.11. Earlier, we had seen Jubilee 45647 *Sturdee* at Leeds, facing the York direction, and we were disappointed that she hadn't taken the TPO forward from there. At York, however, disappointment was to turn to elation.

I have no idea why a train such as the 04.35 departure from York, non-stop to Leeds, actually ran, but I didn't care as *Sturdee*, which had been allocated to a shed

Resulting from the dieselisation of a train that had been expected to be worked by steam, a compensatory tour of York Shed was undertaken on Friday, 13 May. Having travelled with her on the final steam-hauled departure out of Harrogate on the 11.40 to Leeds Central the previous month, B1 61199 is captured in the shed yard.

Just a two-shed locomotive, K1 62046, is silhouetted against the sunlight at 50A's turntable. Arrived from Darlington in 1956, this 17-year-old was withdrawn in February 1967.

Looking for the entire world as if she had been cast aside, this 43-year-old J27 65894 was dispatched to Sunderland later that year, surviving at 52G until September 1967.

And here she is at Grosmont, fifty-six years later, participating in the NYMR 2022 Autumn Gala and about to work a Pickering-bound train with me aboard.

Rusting away in the line of withdrawals was 14-year-old Ivatt 'Flying Pig' 43126. This nomadic Ivatt had been displaced from no fewer than ten previous allocations before arriving here in September 1961.

Ex-London & North Eastern Railway (LNER) 2-6-2 V2 60806 is seen pottering about outside 50A. This 29-year-old was withdrawn that September.

The grandly named B1 61238 *Leslie Runciman* (apparently a well-known Newcastle shipping magnate and prominent politician) at rest at York, her home depot.

Following many years working the fast expresses over the former Great Central line, V2 60831 is seen receiving works attention inside 50A.

After the shed visit, on our return to the station the only steam locomotive we saw there was K1 62028 on station pilot duties.

Having misread the timetable, we became stranded at Wakefield Kirkgate for an hour. It wasn't boring, however, with a seemingly endless stream of WD-hauled freights passing through. Here, 21-year-old home-allocated 2-8-0 90407 is heading westwards with a lengthy load.

Many happy hours were spent here at Bradford Exchange catching steam-worked trains to and from Wakefield, Leeds, Bridlington, Sheffield and Halifax. This atmospheric terminus was razed to the ground in 1973 and was replaced by the current Interchange station ¼ mile to the south. In this shot, Wakefield-allocated Stanier 2-6-4T 42650 is about to work an ECS away to the sidings.

Fairburn 42152 makes a dusk departure from Shipley while working the 20.55 Bradford Forster Square to Birmingham New Street. She would relinquish her train at Leeds City to a Peak DL.

I'd never heard of before – 55C: Farnley Junction – had been turned and worked it. These one-off nocturnal and early morning trains were to become much appreciated by us steam-haulage bashers – sleep deprivation had its rewards.

Back to normality and following a fruitless trip to Hull for an 'expected B1' to Doncaster and some spent time festering at Wakefield Westgate, at least some of her sisters were caught on the Bradford Exchange portions. The Forster Square portions were monopolised by Manningham's LMS tanks.

Paul and I then went our own ways at 20.00. At Bradford, he decided to wait for the 22.00 Huddersfield departure which was booked for Wakefield's Jubilee 45694 *Bellerophon*, while I headed to Manchester for the 22.50 GC line overnight for Marylebone. Words that are unable to be printed here were uttered from Paul's mouth the following month when *Bellerophon* worked a Blackpool to Leeds via Copy Pit service which we were both on!

Just two Basingstoke visits were undertaken before once again heading north that month, the highlight being the Lewisham train crash locomotive, 34066 *Spitfire*, which attained a heady 86mph approaching Brookwood on the lightweight Salisbury. With the National Union of Seamen staging what turned out to be thirteen weeks of strikes, this meant the Channel Island boat trains from Waterloo to Weymouth Quay weren't running. The returning 18.48 non-stop Basingstoke to Waterloo was a casualty of this.

Friday, 20 May saw me, this time with Alan, departing Euston on the 23.45 to Barrow. We did not know precisely which trains remained steam-hauled in north-west England and were disappointed at Crewe when a Brush Type 4 backed on.

Matters improved north of Wigan, however. Following a twenty-five-minute delay, we were assisted at the rear by an unidentified Black 5MT, the DL eventually expiring near Standish Junction. Although we knew we were taken forward some time later by steam, it was not until we alighted at Preston that we delightfully discovered that it was 8F 48319, which maxed at 72mph through Balshaw Lane.

As the train arrived into Preston at 05.00 (eighty-five minutes late), we didn't have long for the 05.35 all-stations stopper for Crewe – a train taking an astonishing two hours to cover the 52½ miles, unusually routed via the triangular-platformed Earlestown. This train was a return working of a Crewe South duty and was often used to run in ex-works locomotives – for example, the final steam locomotive overhauled 70013 *Oliver Cromwell* in February 1967 and, the following month, the preserved A4 *Sir Nigel Gresley*.

The following morning, Saturday, 14 May, saw us collect a ride behind Farnley Junction's Jubilee 45647 *Sturdee*, seen here after arrival at Leeds City with the 04.35 ex-York. Catches such as this (it was, after all, 05.15 hours!) made all those sleep-deprived, nocturnal adventures worthwhile.

Neville Hill-allocated Fairburn 42196 arrives into Leeds City on an ECS working. This refugee from Scotland had arrived at the NER in October 1963. She was transferred to Low Moor upon 55H's closure to steam on 12 June, which enabled me to catch her on a Wakefield to Bradford portion six days later.

Later that same morning and working tender-first, Normanton-allocated Ivatt 2-6-0 43098 heads south through Wakefield Westgate on an engineer's train.

Minutes later and Low Moor's WD 2-8-0 90723 hurries a train of condemned vehicles through Wakefield Westgate.

It really was a WD 'heaven'. Storming up the bank with a northbound coal train at Wakefield Westgate, 21-year-old Vulcan Foundry-built WD 90699 lets everyone around know she's coming through.

A short time later and 90699 is seen again returning south with some empties. Built in 1945, she was bought by BR in 1950 and allocated to Royston. Transferred to 55E in September 1964, she saw out NER steam, lasting until its demise in October 1967.

At Wakefield Westgate, Low Moor-allocated B1 61386 has arrived light engine from 56A to work the Bradford Exchange portion off the 10.20 King's Cross to Leeds Central. These 17-mile, three-coach services were a godsend to chasers such as me – providing runs with these increasingly rare Thompson-designed locomotives. Indeed, by the year's end most of them had either been transferred away from West Riding sheds or withdrawn.

Saturday, 21 May saw me arrive at Chester General from Crewe en route to a bash on the Shrewsbury to Birkenhead trains. Seen arriving with the 07.40 'Club Train', Llandudno to Manchester Exchange, is Holyhead's 44770. As if to justify the versatility of the class, I had caught a run with her off piste in the Bradford area eight days previously.

Shunting in the sidings to the north of the station, Birkenhead-allocated 9F 92082 rests between activities. She was a casualty of the shed's closure to steam in November 1967.

One of three remaining Jinties at 6A, veteran 40-year-old Fowler 47389, is on station pilot duty, perhaps unaware of her impending withdrawal four days later.

After that we bashed the steam-saturated Shrewsbury to Chester General to Birkenhead Woodside services, a reliable source of locomotives from a variety of LMR sheds right up to their cessation in March 1967. In particular, the 15-mile Birkenhead leg from Chester was always monitored as either a Chester Standard 4MT of the 76xxx class or a Birkenhead tank of either Fairburn or Stanier variety was turned out. Presumably, with the mainstay of Birkenhead's workload being the 9F-worked freight services, the 8H crews relished working these lightweight, six-vehicle trains and some high-speed runs were recorded over the Wirral peninsular flatlands en route. The returning overnight train to the Smoke was, once again, the 22.50 Manchester to Marylebone, which was disappointingly worked to Guide Bridge on this occasion by a Type 2 Sulzer.

Back then, you were either a Beatles or Rolling Stones fan. With 'Paint It Black' hitting the top spot, I was definitely one of the latter, even seeing them at the first ever free concert at Hyde Park in 1969 – albeit from halfway up a tree!

Saturday, 28 May saw me make a concerted effort to catch Eastleigh and Bournemouth tanks and Moguls on the New Forest stopping services. Although that part of the plan was unsuccessful, I did manage to catch a Tyseley Black 5MT on the northbound York line and nab my final 'required' SR-allocated Standard 5MT, 73002, on an Eastleigh local.

On the final day that May, I was to be found boarding the 17.09 Basingstoke commuter train at Waterloo not paying much attention to the change of platform announcement concerning the 17.00 Exeter train. Upon leaning out of the leading vehicle, I realised that because of a Warship DL failure, the Exeter was steam-worked that night. An immediate decision involving a hectic dash enabled me to board the 17.00 train seconds before departure – a 66½-mile outing to Andover being a change to the norm. Ascertaining the power at the Woking stop, it was only my final 'required' Bulleid Light Pacific 34002 *Salisbury*. Just one remaining Bulleid to get now: Merchant 12.

Saturday, 28 May at Eastleigh, 70D's sole-surviving Ivatt, 41319, struggles through with a Southampton Docks-bound transfer freight. She was to be reallocated to Nine Elms in April 1967, spending her final days amongst more mundane ECS trains working the 'Kenny Belle'.

Arriving on the SR (Bricklayer's Arms) in December 1959, this Standard 4MT 80083 was transferred to Eastleigh three years later. Here, that same Saturday at Brockenhurst, she is calling with the 12.50 Southampton Terminus to Bournemouth Central three-coach stopper.

JUNE

THE ALNWICK ADVENTURE
NORTHUMBERLAND, CARLISLE & BLACKPOOL

That one remaining Bulleid I 'required', 35012 *United States Lines*, fell into my lap the following evening when she was turned out for the 17.30 ex-Waterloo. So that was that: all the SR allocation of main-line locomotives had now been scratched. The Standard tanks and Moguls could, and indeed did, wait. Every weekend of that 1966 summer was applied to prioritising steam 'oop north'.[2]

Enticed by the use of Stockport-allocated locomotives, the shed not now having any booked passenger work, I was to be found on Saturday, 4 June aboard the LCGB-organised 'Fellsman Rail Tour'. Following EL haulage from Euston to Liverpool Lime Street, Brit 4 *William Shakespeare* took the train via St Helens and Preston to Quintinshill, ably assisted by the unique Stephenson link-equipped Black 5MT 44767 from Carnforth with 87½mph being enjoyed down Shap. The location of Quintinshill is, of course, where the worst railway accident in British history occurred in 1915 – over 200 perished because of errors made by two signalmen.

Returning via Ais Gill to Crewe with Jubilees *Kolhapur* and *Bahamas*, the fun then started. With the overhead line equipment down along the Trent Valley, a Type 4 DL took us via Bescot to Rugby. This resulted in a 203-minute-late arrival, at 00.53 into Euston.

I decided to make the most of this unexpected scenario and walked across London to Waterloo, fortunately meeting no 'Strangers in the Night' (a Frank

---

2 My final SR-allocated 76xxx was caught just nine days before the end, in July 1967.

My first rail tour away from SR metals was 'The Fellsman' on Saturday, 4 June. Here, at Liverpool Lime Street ex-'Golden Arrow' Brit, Stockport-allocated 70004 *William Shakespeare* prepares to work the 135-mile leg to Quintinshill.

The travel ticket for the above-mentioned tour.

Sinatra song hitting the top spot that week), where, because of Bournemouth line engineering work in connection with electrification, all the services were diverted over a myriad of routes. That morning's 03.15 Waterloo to Southampton Terminus was diverted via the Guildford New Line, Pompey Direct and Fareham – this *Yeovil*-hauled train deposited me at Eastleigh at 05.20.

Another diversionary route, between Alton and Winchester, was also in the mix that day and having backtracked to Woking for the *Whimple*-worked 09.33 Waterloo to Bournemouth excursion train, I was disappointed to collect pilotage over 'The Alps' by a Crompton DL, despite most of my mates enjoying steam assistance that day on other diverted trains. With the up-line unaffected, I returned to London via Basingstoke.

Monday, 13 June was a swelteringly hot day for my sole daytime visit to the ex-GC that month. I took the 14.38 out of Marylebone, changing at Rugby Central onto Banbury's 44860-worked 17.20 starter for Nottingham Victoria. With just weeks to go before closure, Ashby Magna was now unstaffed, and I took a few photographs of the station and the almost empty nearby M1 for

For novelty value, having travelled over 'The Alps' on the diverted 09.33 Waterloo to Bournemouth Central train on Sunday, 5 June, I alighted at the newly opened (January 1966) Southampton Airport Station. While waiting for my returning London train, Light Pacific 34026 *Yes Tor* is seen arriving there with the 10.30 Waterloo to Weymouth. The station was renamed Southampton Airport Parkway in May 1994.

By travelling on the 17.20 ex-Rugby Central, I could only make it as far north as here at Ashby Magna without missing the final southbound London train of the day. Note the near empty M1 in the background.

The end is nigh – a closure notice on Ashby Magna Station. The deed was carried out that September.

posterity while awaiting the returning 20.25 Marylebone arrival. What a waste of a railway line, driven by the retrenchment-minded BR which had been hamstrung by the political need for profitability. The line would have been an idea alternative to the congested WCML.

Even though I had cleared the SR main-line steam locomotives for haulage, I still made some weeknight visits to Basingstoke. Of the three visits the following week, Driver Cummings (70A) excelled himself, perhaps prompted by some beer money collected among us for him at Waterloo, achieving 85½mph with *Whimple* on the 15th and 93mph on the 16th with *Lyme Regis*. The train was of course the lightweight 18.38 Salisbury to Waterloo and, although we weren't to know it then, with the racing section between Hook and Brookwood being fettled for the Bournemouth electrics, many three-figure speeds were to be enjoyed over it in the months ahead.

Word among us enthusiasts was that the 3-mile-long Alnwick branch, from the ECML Alnmouth Station, was worked by Peppercorn-designed K1s. None

A wonderful Waterloo rush-hour scene on Thursday, 16 June, with Unmodified Pacific 34015 *Exmouth* on the 17.41 Basingstoke stopper and Battle of Britain 34071 601 *Squadron* departing with the 17.30 for Bournemouth Central. The flats in the distance, offering attractive views of departing trains, were, to the residents' annoyance, much frequented during the mid-1960s, with verbal abuse often being encountered.

of us had been up to this isolated (from other steam train-saturated areas) branch and so Alan and I took a gamble and headed there on the overnight 23.45 out of King's Cross on Friday, 17 June.

Opened in 1850, the original terminus of Alnwick was relocated closer to the town itself in 1887 and a somewhat circuitous line to Coldstream opened in the same year because the Duke of Northumberland did not want intrusion over his land. While passenger services over the latter route ceased as early as 1930 and the through-trains from Newcastle to Alnwick were in the hands of DMUs, the infrequent shuttle trains to Alnmouth were indeed steam operated.

Little did we know that it was the final day of Tweedmouth-resourced steam services – a resplendent (Master Neverers Association (MNA)-cleaned[3]) 62011 being thoroughly appreciated by us. We subsequently learnt, many months later, courtesy of the LCGB *Bulletin* magazine, that the afternoon services were powered by a 9F – but then again, it would have been a lengthy wait and with the superior attraction of numerous, albeit short-haul, steam services in the West Riding, we headed there as quick as the train service allowed us.

All services over the branch went DMU after that weekend – the line did not survive Beeching's axe and was closed in January 1968. Fortunately, the trainshed and main buildings still exist, having been converted into a large bookshop, and the Aln Valley Preservation Society are operating trains over a short section of track east of the A1 motorway.

Arriving into Leeds just before midday, we caught a Manningham tank-powered train into Bradford's Forster Square Station then walked to the Exchange for a run with Mirfield's Blackie 45208. Wonderfully, a 'Flying Pig' and two named B1s made up for the dearth of steam mileage that weekend. It was nicely rounded off with the 22.50 'beds' from Manchester Central to Marylebone and at least Trafford Park sent out a 'required' 45239 for the 10½ miles to Guide Bridge.

Of the three Basingstoke visits the following week the only item of note was Tyseley's 45349 on the 15.50 ex-Weymouth. Was this borrowed by the SR having failed off the York line perhaps? The airwaves later that week saw The Beatles' 'Paperback Writer' reaching top spot.

---

3 A group of photographers who travelled the country cleaning steam locomotives (for photographic purposes) when working 'last' trains.

With no internet back then, we enthusiasts only had our own grapevine, often awash with unsubstantiated rumours, to work on. One of them was that Tweedmouth-allocated K1s worked the Alnwick to Alnmouth shuttles. So, on Saturday, 18 June, Alan and I made the lengthy journey to this Northumberland outpost to investigate. Wonderfully, 2-6-0 62011, seen here at Alnmouth with the 07.50 Alnwick departure, was that day's power.

We didn't know it was the final day of the steam-worked shuttles. Here 62011, specifically cleaned up by the MNA, having run round the two-vehicle train, backs down at Alnwick onto the 08.09 Alnmouth departure. All services went DMU the following Monday and the branch closed in January 1968.

Later that same Saturday, at Bradford Exchange, Mirfield-allocated 5MT 45208 readies herself for the 17-mile journey to Wakefield Westgate with the 13.05 portion for King's Cross. She was to be transferred to Low Moor that December and was withdrawn at the cessation of NER steam on 1 October 1967.

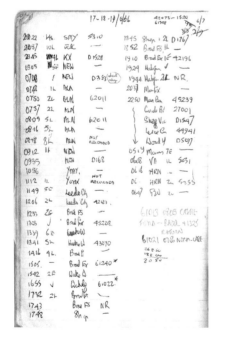

The notebook extract for the 17–19 June outing.

Don't ask me how, but I had surmised that the remaining NER Jubilee locomotives' only passenger duties would be on the summer Saturday holiday extras (retrospectively, I was correct, the one exception being the all-year-round 02.00 Sheffield to Leeds), and to this end I homed in on those short-dated, wavy-line timetabled trains that summer.

The first one I selected was the 13.25 Blackpool North to Bradford Exchange. Having travelled north, on this occasion with Paul, on the 23.45 Barrow 'kippers' out of Euston and alighted at Preston, the twelve intermediate hours were occupied by catching six steam locomotives, which included a brief visit to Chester. You couldn't get any briefer than the connection made that morning. We arrived at 09.03 on the 07.40 Manchester Exchange to Llandudno, raced over the footbridge and jumped on the 07.40 Llandudno to Manchester Exchange as it was about to depart at 09.05. I was fairly certain that obesity would never be an issue for me with exertions such as that, along with the walks across Manchester and London during those frenetic days of chasing steam.

A regular Brit-worked service was the 10.47 from Preston to Barrow (subsequently for the 13.46 to Euston, which she was to work to Crewe) seen here awaiting departure on Saturday, 25 June with ex-ER 70005 *John Milton*.

We then headed to Blackpool, regrettably encountering several wavy-lined trains formed by DMUs en route. This highlights the unpredictability of these short-dated trains as regards the chances of them being steam operated. We waited with expectancy at a station, wires pulled, semaphore lowered and eye-balling the horizon for a wisp of smoke. Being very much hit and miss, it was all part and parcel of the scene at the time and I wouldn't have traded such an experience for the world.

Having arrived at Blackpool's North Station unaware of the farcical regulation tickets that were required (there were just two of us in the first two coaches!), we made an unplanned visit to the booking office, which nearly caused us to miss the train. Luckily, we boarded it with just minutes to go.

Much to Paul's chagrin (see page 65), it was powered by Wakefield's 45694 *Bellerophon*. It was a wonderful two-hour journey via the then freight-only route via Copy Pit and was thoroughly enjoyed. It was of necessity to lean out of the window when passing non-stop through Preston to bellow out, 'Look what we are behind!' to fellow envious enthusiasts congregating at the platform ends.

After participating once more on the delightful Bradford portions, we made our way to Manchester for my first of many journeys on the 'Belfast Boat Express' – Carnforth's 'pet', the now preserved 45025, being that night's power. Having maxed at a very hot 33°C during the day, it was a pleasant walk across Manchester that evening to the Central Station. With no trams back then, I had to rely on Shanks' pony, acquiring in the process an intimate knowledge of the city streets.

And so, this turned out to be my sixth and final occasion aboard the memorable 22.50 Manchester to Marylebone 'beds', followed by a walk across the deserted London streets. A journey that can no longer be recreated over land that has long since been utilised for housing, industrial estates and motorways. The memories still resonate with me.

Travelling over to Blackpool and one of the nine remaining NER-allocated Jubilees, 45694 *Bellerophon*, brews up at Blackpool North about to work the 13.25 Bradford Exchange/ Leeds Central departure via Copy Pit.

Later that same day, and in the gathering gloom, Carnforth's 'pet' Black 5MT 45025 departs Bolton Trinity Street with the 20.55 'Belfast Boat Express' from Manchester Victoria to Heysham Harbour. She was regularly turned out for the BBE and, having worked one of the many rail tours on the final day of steam in August 1968, has survived into preservation at the Strathspey Railway.

A notebook extract for that June weekend jaunt.

A glorious summer's evening, Wednesday, 29 June sees 34100 *Appledore* departing Basingstoke while working the 18.00 Waterloo to Salisbury. She was a former South Eastern (SR) locomotive and, upon being allocated to Salisbury, was, as were all of their Bulleids, kept in excellent condition until the end.

This is to certify that

Mr. K. WIDDOWSON

has been admitted to THE LOCO-MOTIVE CLUB OF GREAT BRITAIN

as from 30.6.66 and is entitled to participate in its activities subject to the conditions of the constitution.

J. Cramp

Hon. General Secretary.

Membership No. 2422

Annual Subscription paid

To:— 31 DEC 1966 /c.

31 DEC 1967

31 DEC 1968

Membership of the Locomotive Club of Great Britain (LCGB) qualified for a reduced fare on their tours and a percentage reduction on a great many publications.

JUBILEE JOY
BARNSLEY, BRIDLINGTON & ABERDEEN

It's difficult to recall, all these years later, whether a weekend outing was planned or – this is more than likely – we went where the 'required' locomotives took us. Making the most of a valuable day's leave on Friday, 1 July, I headed for the 13.27 FO Manchester Victoria to Edinburgh Waverley. As can be seen from my accompanying notebook extract, without leaving your compartment, this was a six-locomotive train if you included the assisting locomotives up Shap and Beattock Banks. With a fifty-one-minute-late arrival, mainly due to awaiting the return of the Fairburn tank which had banked a preceding freight at Beattock, Bob and I could only make Kirkcaldy (rather than Dundee) for the 19.45 FO Aberdeen to York. This steam-worked, short-dated train over the Forth Bridge to Edinburgh was another where – unknown to us – regulation tickets were required. It was only upon showing our BR identity cards that we were allowed through the barrier, having located a nearby chippy to satisfy our hunger – the train was already at the platform, eager to depart.

It was just as well the train terminated at York, where we planned to alight, because we were shaken awake by station staff wanting to send it to the sidings. Rubbing the sleep from our eyes, a resplendent Jubilee *Alberta* awaited us on the 04.35 Leeds City departure.

Heading over to Bradford Exchange and unsure as to whether the 08.20 Bridlington train was steam-worked, we waited for the stock to arrive and the tell-tale smoke from the front before dashing to the booking office for tickets.

Fortune shone upon us once more with Low Moor's (only) 'pet' Jubilee 45565 *Victoria* taking us the 92 miles through the flatlands adjacent to the Humber estuary before taking the Hull-avoiding curve to the East Coast resort. With no time for a visit to the beach, we headed to Scarborough for the 13.35 Manchester departure which, although it was powered by a Black 5, was annoyingly piloted to York by a Brush Type 4.

Alighting from this train at Wakefield, we then made our way to Sheffield for the 11.55 Yarmouth to Manchester – this short-dated summer Saturday-only train was powered from there by Newton Heath's 44846. With Driver Fieldhouse explaining his hair-raising speeds through the tortuous Hope Valley route (we maxed at 80mph through Bamford) as wanting 'to get home to Oldham in time for his tea', we made up an astonishing eighteen minutes on the schedule, arriving eight minutes early.

We then crossed the Pennines to Huddersfield, making a very tight connection onto the Poole to Bradford train, which was luckily running twelve minutes late and had *Sturdee* working it that day. We were assisted from Greetland Junction by one of Low Moor's Fairburn tanks before finally leaving the West Riding area that evening on the one-Brake Second Corridor (BSK) 22.00 Bradford Exchange to Huddersfield.

This train usefully connected into the 21.50 TPO York to Aberystwyth, which had a two-vehicle detachment for Manchester Exchange at Stalybridge. With the main train having departed Stalybridge we could see, in the distance, a locomotive silhouetted against the night sky, slowly coming towards us. Once the identity of the locomotive became visible, cries of either joy or disappointment resounded from us.

Usually a Patricroft-allocated Caprotti Standard 5MT or, less often, a Newton Heath Black 5MT, it always worked the two-vehicle portion tender first. I believe it was a part of the Exchange Station pilot duty and, to boot, by a quirk of diagramming was steam-worked on a Sunday morning only.

Picture the scene. While the majority of our fellow youths were enjoying the night life – it was, after all, a quarter past midnight in the Manchester streets over which we were running, most of the 8-mile route being on viaducts – here we were, tired, unkempt but taking in the atmosphere of a steam train. On this occasion, it was maxing at 52mph en route. By window-hanging and soaking up an atmosphere that was soon to disappear, we were taking in a part of history. What were they doing? Getting wasted on drink and fighting each other, vying to attract the opposite sex – activities we could all enjoy *after* steam had finished!

It's Saturday, 2 July, and Low Moor-allocated, Derby-built Fairburn 42177 is seen storming up the incline out of Bradford Exchange with the three-coach 08.20 portion for Wakefield Westgate, where it will be placed on the rear of the main train from Leeds Central to King's Cross. These photographs were taken from the much heavier 08.20 Bridlington departure, the train crews and signalmen coordinating their climbs at lineside photographers' requests. Such was the camaraderie between enthusiasts and railwaymen.

Low Moor's sole Jubilee, 45565 *Victoria*, is seen at Bridlington having worked the 92 miles from Bradford Exchange. This was to be her Indian summer, withdrawal coming in January 1967.

Finally, we boarded the 01.00 Manchester Exchange for Wigan North Western. This Patricroft-resourced, sleeping-car portion train, with one BSK for any stop-outs, was to be frequented by me on a mind-boggling forty-eight occasions before it ceased being steam-worked in May 1968. That was it then. We southern-based enthusiasts awaited the 02.53 Euston train while our northern compatriots went home to their warm beds.

On this occasion, instead of heading to my Kent home after arrival into London, I walked over to Waterloo and had a much-anticipated fry-up at a café adjacent to the Bull Ring, before heading onto the concourse, only to learn that the V2 that had been booked to work the 'Green Arrow Rail Tour' had failed at Nine Elms. With the substituted power being an 'unrequired' Light Pacific *Salisbury*, I disappointedly made my way home. Fatigue caught up with me that 'Sunny Afternoon' (The Kinks' hit at the time) because I fell asleep in a deckchair in the garden and suffered some serious sunburn.

Following two uneventful Basingstoke outings during the week, Friday 8 July saw me departing London on the 21.20 St Pancras to Glasgow Central in yet another attempt to catch a run with one of the fast-dwindling number

A notebook extract depicting a somewhat hectic weekend.

of Gresley-designed V2s. The other objective, that of reaching Aberdeen by steam, was also yet to be achieved because of the late running of the overnight Anglo-Scottish trains the previous summer.

The train had changed locomotives at a junction outside of Leeds City Station, so it wasn't until Carlisle that the Jubilee that had taken us over Ais Gill was identified. It was Holbeck's stalwart *Kolhapur*, which worked the 229 miles from Leeds to Glasgow throughout.

Although we were thirty minutes late into Glasgow Central Station it was an easy walk across to Buchanan Street for the A4 *Kingfisher*-worked 08.25 'Grampian Express'. I could have stayed aboard to Aberdeen, but I presume the need for a run with a V2 took preference. Having alighted at Stirling, my travelling companion once again being George and I made our way to Dunfermline to 'intercept' the short-dated summer extras on the Dundee to Edinburgh line. With no V2s in circulation once again, we took a Black 5-worked train over the subsequently closed route via Glenfarg (now under the M90) to Perth and boarded the 11.00 Glasgow to Aberdeen, which had one of St Rollox's Caprottis in charge. The rumour mill had gone into overdrive with the news that V2 60813 was to work forward from Dundee, but, disappointingly, one of 62B's B1s was turned out. At least I was now, at last, steaming into Aberdeen. With the weather throughout that month maxing at 30°C, the cooling breeze off the North Sea coming through the open windows of the Gresley compartmented coach when running alongside it was most welcome.

The returning 'Granite City Express', the 17.15 Aberdeen to Glasgow Buchanan Street, was an unbelievable and unforgettable experience. Mile after mile via the Forfar cut-off, *Kingfisher* hit the mid to high 70s, with a maximum speed of 85½mph being obtained through Coupar Angus.

Sadly, serving very few locations of population, all services were diverted via Dundee in 1967 and the line was closed. So now, with last year's 'beds', the 20.25 Perth to Marylebone, having disappeared from the 1966 timetable, what was the steamiest way home?

The answer lay with 'The Northern Irishman', the 22.00 Stranraer Harbour to Euston. I had planned to intercept this train at Girvan, having travelled out of Glasgow Central on the 21.00 Stranraer departure, but due to a partial failure on the DMU, I only made it to Ayr. It was perhaps fortuitous that this happened because reference to the timetable sometime afterwards showed that 'The Northern Irishman' would only call at Girvan upon 'prior notice being given to the stationmaster'. I can picture the scene, with the DMU having stopped in the Stranraer-bound platform while the London train passed through, completely stranding me for the night.

Although I appreciated getting a 'required' Brit 17 *Arrow* on the boat train on its extra 43-mile route via Mauchline, the Port Road having closed in May the previous year, I lost out on the Caprotti Standard pilot, which came off at Ayr. That particular one never graced my *Locoshed* book.

Following two further Basingstoke visits during the week, Friday, 15 July saw me once more head for the NER in my quest to obtain runs with the remaining handful of Jubilees. Word had got round about the overnight Calder Valley mail trains being steam-worked, so as part of the assemblage of enthusiasts, I got off the *Achilles*-worked 02.00 from Sheffield at Normanton and hit the famed Calder Valley circuit.

As detailed in the table opposite, I participated in this wonderful scenario on five occasions that year – and indeed, on many more during 1967, with the 02.10 ex-York remaining steam-worked from Halifax as late as May 1968.

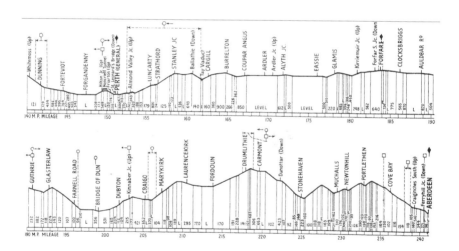

Gradient profile of the Forfar cut-off route.

Location	Arrival	Departure	Train	16 July	23 July	27 July	31 July	8 Oct
Sheffield Mid.	--	02.00	For Leeds City	45697 (55A)	45675 (55A)	45675 (55A)	45675 (55A)	DL
Normanton	02.52	03.10	02.10 York–Manchester Vic.	61189 (56F)	--[4]	61022 (56A)	61388 (56F)	42204 (56A)
Halifax	--	04.38	--	44890 (9D)	--	45101 (9D)	45336 (9D)	44949 (9D)
Hebden Bridge	05.05	05.28	04.20 Manchester Vic.–York	45062 (9J)	45385 (8F)	44962 (8F)	45385 (8F)	44679 (8F)
Normanton	--	--	--	61319 (50A)	61199 (50A)	61019 (50A)	61019 (50A)	42149 (55E)
Castleford Ctl	07.15	08.05	For Blackpool North	44910 (8L)	45739 (56A)	44694 (56F)	--	--
Brighouse	08.51	--	--	--	--	--	--	--

Shed codes: 8L = Aintree (Liverpool); 8F = Springs Branch (Wigan); 9D = Newton Heath (Manchester); 9J = Agecroft (Manchester); 50A = York; 55A = Leeds Holbeck; 55E = Normanton; 56A = Wakefield; 56F = Low Moor (Bradford).

Starting off with the 02.00 out of Sheffield, a cross-platform connection at Normanton led us (there were often up to two dozen of us) to the York to Manchester train. Provided with just one BSK, the two-hour journey to Hebden Bridge (nowadays a tourist magnet, having been the location of the hit TV police drama *Happy Valley*) was the furthest west one could travel before changing onto the opposite way working, and often led to fatigue and sleeping during the lengthy station stops – the all-pervading steam heating assisted matters. Before falling into the land of nod, however, news of locomotive transfers and shed and route closures were bandied around – back then, it was the only method of communication about the constantly changing steam scene, and it was most valuable. With information duly exchanged, sleep was then attempted – but with six to a compartment, this was not always very successful.

Fortunately, Dave, who although I believe he resided somewhere in the Midlands had acquired the nickname 'Mytholmroyd', was sufficiently alert and would walk down the corridor banging on the compartment windows to wake

---

4 Connection missed: 42204 (56A), taken on 04.25 to Wakefield Kirkgate and 43070 (56A) on the 05.15 to Barnsley and 06.10 return.

us up when passing through said station, it being just minutes away from our destination. At Hebden Bridge, the porter, who was suddenly overwhelmed with such a large contingent alighting there, gave up any attempt to check tickets, uttering, 'You've all got rovers then?' Twenty minutes later and we were heading back east, looking forward to the traction change at Normanton. The foreman there was often liable to turn out a locomotive from a wide variety of classes for the remaining 24 miles to York.

Not that we were going all the way there – just nine minutes later, we all alighted at Castleford Station and invaded the adjacent bus depot's staff canteen, which was affectionally known as the 'beanery'. The said food was wolfed down in large quantities. Why the rush? Well, during the summer months, an 08.05 Blackpool-destined train departed from there, which we all boarded before dispersing away to various destinations according to our 'needs'.

In my case, having heard that *Alberta* was working the 09.15 Leeds to Llandudno, I, along with Scottish enthusiast George once again, headed for Huddersfield to catch her – oodles of new steam track, including freight lines in the Warrington area, being the incentive. Just prior to boarding the train at Huddersfield, however, we learnt from other enthusiasts that Jubilee *Bihar & Orissa* was on that day's Bradford to Poole (on which she would work to Nottingham) and as both of us 'required' her, we made immediate plans to travel to Sheffield to catch her returning run.

Having alighted at Rhyl, we caught a Standard 5MT-worked train back to Manchester Exchange and walked across to Piccadilly, before taking an EL ride through Woodhead Tunnel to Sheffield Victoria. We had just eleven minutes to race across to the Midland Station with bags and cameras – I am certain our hobby kept us fit! Just making it, *Bihar & Orissa* took us the 53 glorious miles of undulating gradients through to Bradford assisted from Greetland Junction by one of the few remaining NER-allocated Stanier tanks, Wakefield's 42664. It was well worth the effort – particularly as 45581 was withdrawn the following month.

So, the same plan as two weeks previously then took effect. Although the 22.00 out of Bradford was wonderfully worked by a B1, the Stalybridge portion was DL and, would you believe it, Standard 5MT 73006 (caught in north Wales just twelve hours previously) worked the 01.00 Manchester to Wigan. Some you win and some you lose! On this occasion, following a three-hour fester on Crewe's platforms and a bus replacement journey between Longport and Longton, I made my way to Leicester for a family get-together.

Having neglected the GC line out of Marylebone over recent weeks, Tuesday, 19 July saw me make amends with 206 steam miles accumulated on a Leicester return trip, with Colwick's 44847 on the 14.38 departure being the sole 'requirement'. There was a noticeable drop in the number of passengers, particularly on the returning 17.15 ex-Nottingham Victoria.

Following two further midweek outings to Basingstoke, on Friday, 22 July, I once again headed to the NER in my quest for runs with the remaining Jubilees. To that end, it was a successful completion with *Hardy* on the 02.00 ex-Sheffield and *Ulster* on the 08.05 ex-Castleford Central.

Matters went awry, however, with *Hardy* standing for nearly thirty minutes, held at signals seemingly in the middle of nowhere. This resulted in all twenty-eight (a census was conducted during the delay) enthusiasts being stranded at Normanton – the Manchester mails NOT being held.

Wandering around the station, we discovered a single coach in one of the bay platforms was to form the 04.25 departure for Rochdale (unadvertised

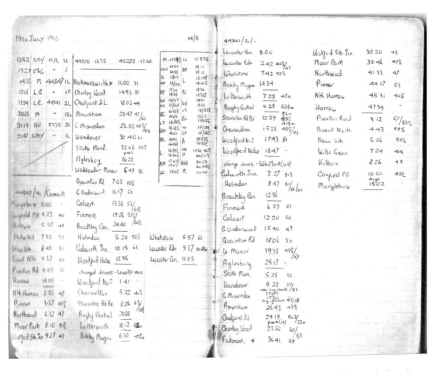

Tuesday, 19 July, and the detailed timings of the two trains caught over ex-GC metals that day.

beyond Wakefield Kirkgate) and in due course, a 56A-allocated Fairburn took us the 3 miles to Wakefield. We had alighted there in the hope that the 05.15 for Barnsley together with the 06.10 return were steam-hauled and, sure enough, 'Flying Pig' 43070 duly performed the honours. The guard, never having seen so many customers on this one-BSK train, didn't bother to check tickets. Just as well, as I doubt whether any of us held valid ones! Arriving back at Wakefield, normality returned to our plans and we all headed to the Castleford 'beanery' for sustenance then obviously away from there with *Ulster*.

Those overnight mail trains were the lifeblood for a chaser such as me. Running over lines dominated during the daytime by DMUs, there were occasions, particularly after the cessation of SR steam in July 1967, that travelling conditions were akin to a London rush hour – full and standing room only. Although I wasn't present at the time, I believe on one occasion a platform seat was placed in a parcels van at Halifax on the 04.38 Manchester departure to accommodate the masses safely.

They were wonderful days – the comradeship, the rivalry, the banter. If only the social media sites that exist today were available back then. With most of us coming from all over the UK, once the common denominator of steam disappeared in August 1968, contact with most of them ceased.

We all had nicknames, with some based on the geographical location they resided at and some 'awarded' by the rest of us. Here are those that I recall (apologies to those I can't): Nobby, Midland Red, Shunter, Lurch, Wild Bill, Jock, The Hat, Whiskers, Prestatyn, Doze, The Squire, The Boy, Clackers, Jo, Pest, Charlie Firmfinger, Lenny, Malphus, Pricy, Wallasey, Penguin and Bedford.

Anyway, back to that July Saturday, and upon embarking on my first daylight trip over Ais Gill with Jubilee *Kolhapur*, I elected to time the train's progress over this most scenic of routes. This 73-mile Settle to Carlisle line was completed by the Midland Railway in 1876 because the company was frustrated with access problems caused by the London & North Western Railway (L&NWR) when forwarding their Scotland-bound passengers over the WCML via Shap. There have been numerous books detailing the problematic construction of it, including the many lives lost within the Irish navvy workforce, so I will concentrate on the journey I made that day.

The progress to Hellifield was unremarkable but upon diverging at Settle Junction, the pyrotechnics from the front of the train commenced. There were now 15 miles to Blea Moor Tunnel. As it was on an uphill ruling gradient of 1 in 100, with speeds never exceeding 35mph, it was necessary to 'window

The Calder Valley Circuit fell down on Saturday, 23 July, due to the late running of the 02.00 from Sheffield. Disappointment turned to jubilation, though, upon chancing across the one-coach 'Flying Pig'-worked 05.15 Wakefield Kirkgate to Barnsley, Wakefield's 43070, seen here about to return with the 06.10 departure.

Lady luck shone on me later that same day when my final 'required' NER-allocated Jubilee, 45739 *Ulster*, was turned out by Wakefield to work the 08.05 from Castleford Central to Blackpool North.

hang' (which nowadays is only possible on preserved railways) to witness the struggle the Jubilee had with her eight-coach train. The annoyance of soot, grit and smuts was willingly endured to witness the sheer power, noise and visual effect of a steam locomotive working hard, her sounds resonating off the surrounding hills.

All of this was enjoyed while passing through the spectacular scenery on offer. Having travelled over the famed Ribblehead Viaduct and through the 1½-mile-long Blea Moor Tunnel, it seemed as if we were on the top of the world when passing through Dent Station – England's highest at 1,150ft above sea level.

We were journeying on the backbone of England and having passed the peak of the line at Ais Gill, the long descent, interrupted by a call at Appleby, began. Speeds were now in the high 60s and low 70s – the fireman perhaps relaxing a little. If any reader has yet to travel over the line, which was saved from closure

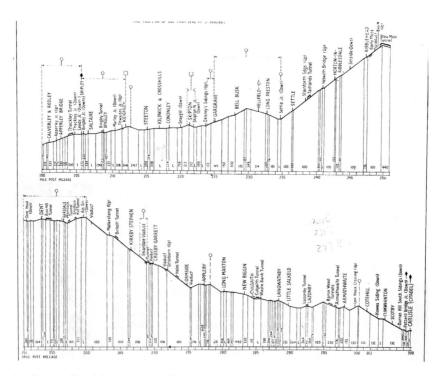

Gradient profile of the Settle to Carlisle route.

in the 1980s by Transport Minister Michael Portillo, then I recommend it – a great many steam excursions travel over it every year.

After arriving into Carlisle bang on time at 13.00 and with the objective of catching all the NER-allocated Jubilees having been accomplished, I now turned my attention to catching runs with all the remaining Britannia locomotives. After a superb run over Shap with Brit 32 *Tennyson* and a couple of locals in the Preston area, the 01.00 Manchester Exchange was again utilised to return to the Smoke. In the charts, Chris Farlowe's 'Out of Time' was ousted from the top spot by The Troggs' 'With a Girl Like You'.

With temperatures that week peaking at 35°C, and following two Basingstoke visits, I, lemming-like, headed for Scotland in my quest for a run with a V2 on Friday, 29 July. I was thwarted, however, by the ninety-five-minute-late running of the 21.20 ex-St Pancras, when a drunken army trainee cadet put his arm through a corridor train window at Chesterfield and the coach, inconveniently situated in the middle of the train, had to be taken out at Sheffield. I aborted the attempt and alighted at Carlisle.

The compensatory run of ten 'required' locomotives on the WCML wavy-lined summer Saturday extras, together with a Fairburn tank and a 'Flying Pig' on Wigan locals was, however, much appreciated. I was obliviously unaware of the historic importance of England winning the World Cup, beating Germany 4–2 that day.

So, once again, for the third consecutive week I took the 01.00 Manchester to Wigan. This train was platformed by 23.00 for the sleeping car customers to bed down for the night. Having been steam-heated from then on, the compartments of the one-BSK provided a very warm, sleep-inducing environment. Bearing in mind that most of the enthusiasts aboard had been out for at least two nights, many struggled to stay awake for the Wigan stop. On one occasion in 1967, on my own with no one to wake me, I found myself at Carlisle and had to phone my office to request an unplanned day's leave. I was fortunate in having an understanding manager!

It's the 18.00 Waterloo to Salisbury, and Basingstoke witnesses the smoky departure of Battle of Britain 34089 *602 Squadron* on Wednesday, 27 July. This train had been an Exeter service until the WR takeover and dieselisation of them in September 1964. It was turned over to Class 33/TCs ten weeks later.

It's 06.30 in the morning at Carlisle and having travelled overnight on a Jubilee-operated summer Saturday service over Ais Gill, on Saturday 30 July, Brit 70048 *The Territorial Army 1908–1958* is seen arriving with a relief from Euston to Glasgow. I failed to catch a run with this Upperby-allocated Brit even though she was transferred to Kingmoor and not withdrawn until April 1967.

Later that day, and Lostock Hall's Fairburn 42105 departs Leyland with the 16.22 Preston to Wigan North Western stopper.

An example of one of the free passes I qualified for as a BR employee.

BRIT BASHING
CREWE, PRESTON & EDINBURGH

Although two visits to Basingstoke were made during that first week of August, I documented that I had a stinking cold. That was not helped by an hour's delay on the returning 15.50 ex-Weymouth due to a complete air pressure failure at Farnborough signal box causing red lights everywhere.

A missing piece of steam track that I had not travelled over was the 29 miles between Wolverhampton Low Level and Shrewsbury, and as only one train was booked for steam haulage over it, the 15.10 (SX) Paddington to Shrewsbury, a valuable day's leave was taken on Friday, 5 August – the day The Beatles released their *Revolver* album.

To access this train, I travelled out of Waterloo on the 11.30 Bournemouth train, connecting at Basingstoke into the Poole to York. This train turned up with a 'required' Black 5MT 44777,[5] which was promptly failed and was replaced with an SR Standard 5MT after nearly an hour's delay. I learnt a valuable lesson that day – which still applies these days when visiting preserved railways – *never* document a haulage until a movement takes place!

It was a very warm night and after making my way to Crewe, calling in for sausage and chips, I headed to Carlisle having learnt that the overnight Glasgow to Birmingham train, normally attaching a portion from Edinburgh at Carstairs during the summer months, was running separately and, to boot,

---

5   I eventually caught up with her thirteen months later while working out of Manchester Exchange on the 01.00 to Wigan.

was steam-worked south of Carlisle. This 02.08 departure, accessed on this occasion by a crew change stop on an Anglo-Scottish train at 01.30 (but only because someone banged a nearby door arousing me from a deep sleep!), was to prove an addictive starting point for several more WCML Saturday bashes – 141 miles of Brit haulage to Crewe being a perfect aperitif.

At Carlisle, I met George, my Scottish fellow chaser, and we had a First-Class sleep all the way to Crewe. He accompanied me back to Warrington, where we went our separate ways. That was how it was back then – we all had different needs with each *Locoshed* book having different underlinings.

On to Preston and the unnamed Brit 47 was on that day's 10.47 Barrow departure. More mates, from the southern and Birmingham areas, were aboard this train. Bombing up and down the 21 miles between Preston and Lancaster on another two occasions, it was late afternoon when Brit 13 *Oliver Cromwell* meandered through on a non-stop Crewe to Carlisle train having been cautioned by adverse signals at the north end of the platform.

'Wow!' stated Deano, one of my companions, 'That's my last required Brit.' Dashing over to the platform in case it stopped, upon seeing his attempt to catch the train several other chasers, already aboard the train, opened a door to enable him to jump aboard. Although he was successful and without mishap, the guard had seen what had happened and applied the emergency brake – thus allowing all of us to board the train while he remonstrated with the miscreant himself. A stupid and dangerous move, which I don't condone, but which I selfishly benefitted from!

Having arrived at Carlisle at 18.45, I was wondering what to do and where to head for next when I noticed several more experienced enthusiasts crowded around a telephone box. It turned out they were phoning the Kingmoor foreman to ask what was being turned out for the 20.25 Perth departure.

I was completely unaware of the existence of this train, so when they found out it was Brit 6 *Robert Burns* how could I refuse my fifth new member of the class within twenty-four hours? Taking it to Coatbridge Central (where the porter informed us who had won that evening's big boxing fight between Cassius Clay and Brian London), after visiting a nearby chippy and returning on the standing-room-only southbound 'Highlander', we alighted at Carlisle to enjoy a further 141 miles of Brit haulage – the overnight Edinburgh, again running separately, this time with Brit 2 *Geoffrey Chaucer*.

Alighting at Crewe just after 05.30 and expecting a lengthy wait for the Sunday morning London-bound services to commence, within minutes the

Taken by precariously hanging out of the window near Standish Junction, Springs Branch's 45281 is seen on a northbound freight on Saturday, 6 August. She was withdrawn on that shed's closure to steam in December 1967.

seventy-four-minute-late-running 'Northern Irishman' deposited us into Euston at a respectable 09.23. Over 740 steam miles, 515 of which were with six Brits — we were living the dream!

The Beatles' double-sided 'Yellow Submarine/Eleanor Rigby' now took the top spot – holding on to it for four weeks. Following just one Basingstoke visit that Wednesday (was I physically exhausted?), it was off to Scotland once more on Friday, 12 August.

Alan, having spotted a 21.50 Euston to Glasgow relief in the LMR STN publication, steered me 243 Brit miles north of Crewe – *Robert Burns* being assisted up Beattock by the sole member of the Scottish allocation of Standard 4MTs that I was to travel with – home-allocated 76098. Arriving into Glasgow Central one and a half hours late at 07.50, we walked across to Buchanan Street for the 08.25 Aberdeen to find that it was a DL! By default, this led us to catching a 09.08 DMU to Inverkeithing to intercept the summer Saturday extras along the east coast route.

What a result! Just minutes later and V2 60813 turned up on the 09.10 Dundee to Blackpool. After hours of frustrated travel, both this summer and last year, we got 13¼ miles of V2 haulage. It didn't matter how short the journey was or that she achieved a mere 67½mph en route.

We sallied over the Forth Bridge on a high. This iconic bridge took seven years to build and was officially opened by the Prince of Wales (later King Edward VII) in 1890. The total length of the bridge is just over 1½ miles and the three great 361ft-high tower cantilevers rest on granite piers, all linked with metal supports somewhat indicative of a spider's web. Train speeds are limited to 50mph for passenger and 20mph for freight. In July 2015, UNESCO designated the structure as a World Heritage Site and there are plans to add a visitor centre and viewing platform to it.

So, back to 1966, and only like-minded chasers can imagine the euphoria of the catch. Just sixteen minutes later and Standard 5MT 73108 took us on an exhilarating, ear-splitting climb up Cobbinshaw Bank before charging down at a hair-raising 81mph on a Carstairs-bound portion. Unsure as to whether to stay aboard for a DL ride to Carlisle, our minds were made up when a 'required' Black 5MT arrived on a Glasgow-bound train and we jumped aboard.

On arrival into Glasgow Central, we espied a train in Platform 1 at the head of which was a brace of Stanier's finest. It didn't matter where it was going – we were on it.

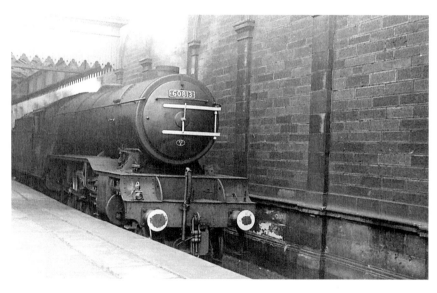

Having been quickly detached from her train at Edinburgh Waverley, a hurried photograph of Dundee's V2 60813 was taken on Saturday, 13 August. After several attempts to travel behind one, I was still in a state of euphoria after catching her from Inverkeithing over the iconic Forth Bridge.

It turned out to be a 13.25 Morecambe-destined train via the Glasgow & South Western (G&SWR) route on which we enjoyed the 116 miles to Carlisle. We didn't have too long to wait at Carlisle for a southbound steam over Shap because a careworn Standard Caprotti 5MT, with steam and smoke emitting from every orifice, was turned out for the following Glasgow to Manchester/ Liverpool train. The driver refused to take the fifteen-vehicle train forward and after two were detached, he managed somehow to coax her to work the 90 miles to Preston before failing her. It was definitely a 'window-hanging' experience, listening to her climb Shap and topping it at a very noisy 32½mph before haring down at a max of 78½mph! For sure, the skills of the crew were tested to the limit that day.

Lostock Hall's Fairburn 42224 was that evening's Blackpool portion loco-motive which, in the 1966 timetable, had its first stop at Lytham St Annes – we gricers having to backtrack to Kirkham & Wesham on a DMU to con-nect into the 21.55 Blackpool North to Liverpool Exchange. This somewhat

The summer Saturday 13.25 Glasgow Central to Morecambe Promenade was a regular double-header – the lengthy train being routed via the gradient-strewn G&SWR. Hurlford's 45490 and Carnforth's 45227 are seen prior to departure, later that day. 45490 was transferred to Motherwell and was withdrawn that December, while 45227 went to Lostock Hall and was withdrawn in January 1968.

inconvenient arrangement was rectified the following year with the outward portion calling at Kirkham, thus allowing a considerable number of us to gather in the adjacent pub before returning into Preston on the Blackpool train. One of my friends, Joe, called the gathering 'a meeting of mateage' because among the partaking of beer, tales were told of the day's catches (or misses!) by all with the banter akin to a foreign language to the bemused regulars.

Returning to that August 1966 visit, cries of 'Not that old rust-bucket!' were to be heard when the Liverpool train rolled in, powered by the Bank Hall's seemingly regular 44809. Changing at Preston, we headed to Manchester for the predictable 01.00 Wigan portion. This 20-mile, thirty-six-minute train was to become the sole source of haulage by Patricroft's Standard 5MTs following the dieselisation of the Manchester to North Wales trains that October.

Was that it for the weekend? I think not. The 02.53 Wigan to Euston, due in at 06.20, was an hour late into Wigan due to a preceding train running into a landslide near Sanquhar. Upon awakening at Rugby, we were informed that we had suffered a one-and-a-half-hour signal stand at Stafford because an engineer's train had derailed. In addition to that, after a derailment the previous day had blocked three of the four lines at Watford, we were 188 minutes late into Euston at 09.28.

Normally, this wouldn't have mattered but we both wanted to travel out of Waterloo on the 09.52 'A2 Commemorative Tour' with the visiting 60532 *Blue Peter*. By positioning ourselves precisely where the exits were on the underground, we made it with three minutes to spare! For sure, the A2 wasn't in the best of health, and having stalled on Honiton Bank followed by an extended visit to Exmouth Junction shed for attention, the hour-and-a-half Salisbury shed visit was negated, with Brit 4 *William Shakespeare* working through from Westbury to Waterloo. We covered 923 steam miles with thirteen locomotives from eight different classes. Oh boy, weren't we the lucky ones!

The following Tuesday, a phone call from Alan alerted me to the fact that Brit 4 *William Shakespeare*, having arrived at Nine Elms on Sunday evening off the A2 rail tour, was to work the 17.23 boat train, Waterloo to Southampton Docks. It was a diagrammed move made by an enthusiast clerk at the Wimbledon office to 'smuggle' the locomotive back to the LMR – the plan being for it to work a 'banana special' from the docks the following day. Normally, this train would have run non-stop to Southampton but to cater for the enthusiast fraternity, it was designated as a relief to the 17.30 – thus calling at Basingstoke, Winchester City and Eastleigh. I'm not sure of the cruise customers' reactions upon being invaded by a deluge of duffle-coated (anoraks had

Visiting A2 60532 *Blue Peter* calls at Salisbury for crew change and water replenishment on Sunday, 14 August. She wasn't a well bunny that day and sat down on Honiton Bank for some time while working this Waterloo to Exeter rail tour.

On returning from Exeter with the same rail tour, Brit 70004 *William Shakespeare* is seen at Westbury taking over the late-running train. She was to work it through to Waterloo rather than just to Salisbury in a bid to regain some time.

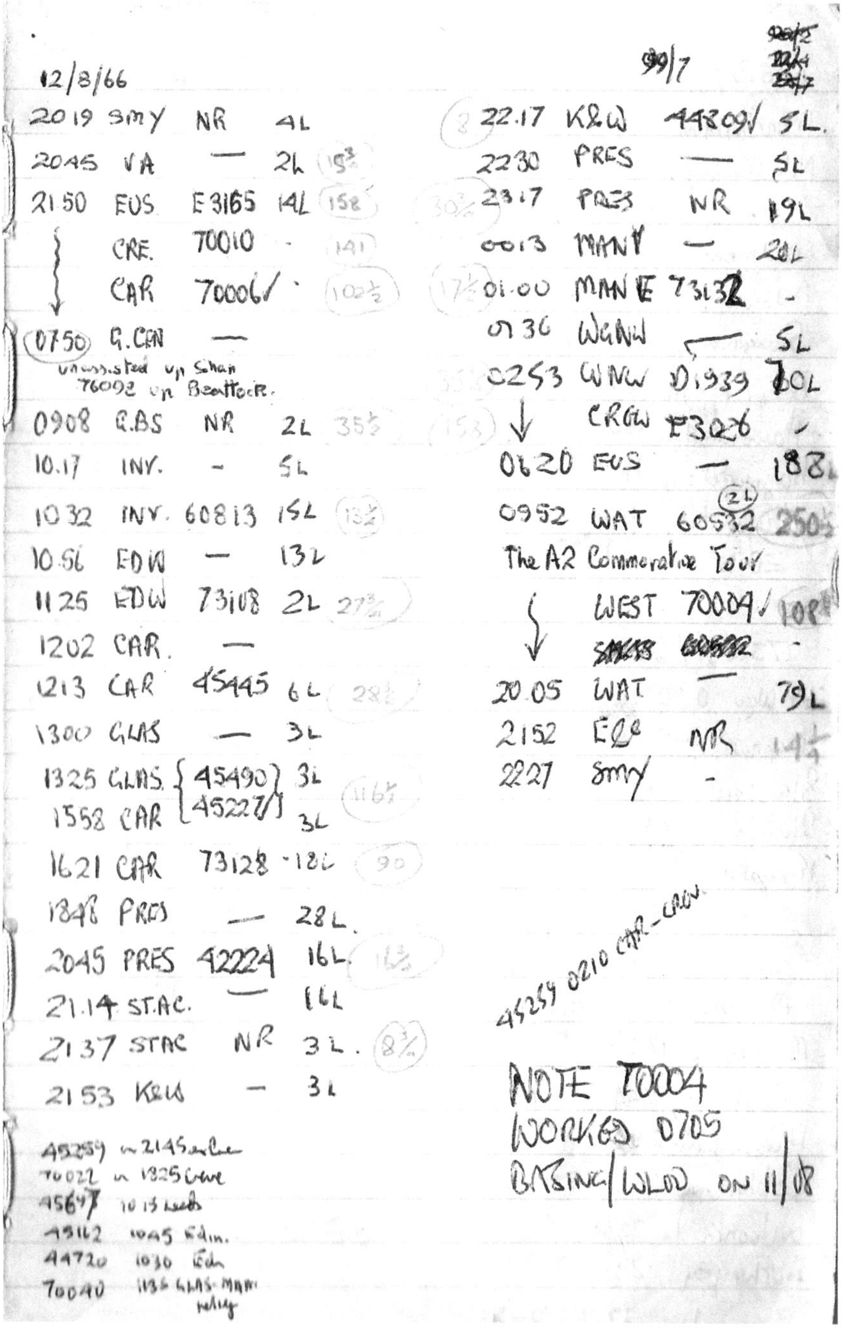

12/8/66

2019 SMY   NR   4L
2045 VA   —   2L (15³)
2150 EUS   E3165 14L (158)
      CRE   70010 ·   (141)
      CAR   70006✓ ·   (102½)
(0750) G.CEN   —
      unassisted up Schan
      76092 up Beattock.
0908 R.BS   NR   2L 35½
10.17 INV.   —   5L
1032 INV. 60813 15L (13½)
10.56 EDW   —   13L
1125 EDW 73108 2L 27½
1202 CAR.   —
1213 CAR 45445 6L 28½
1300 GLAS   —   3L
1325 GLAS { 45490 } 3L (116⅜)
1558 CAR { 45227 } 3L
1621 CAR 73128 ·18L (90)
1848 PRES   —   28L
2045 PRES 42224 16L (11½)
21.14 ST.AC.   —   16L
2137 STAC   NR   3L . (8½)
2153 K&W   —   3L

45259 w 2145 w Car
76022 w 1325 Crwe
45647 10.15 Leeds
45162 1045 Edin.
44720 1030 Edin
76040 1136 GLAS - MAN
      way

99/7

22.17 K&W   44809✓ 5L.
2230 PRES   —   5L
23.17 PRES   NR   19L
0013 MANY   —   20L
01.00 MAN E 73132 ·
0136 WGNW   —   5L
0253 WNW D.939 20L
      ↓ CRGW E3026 ·
0620 EUS   —   188L
0952 WAT 60532 250½
The A2 Commerative Tour
{   WEST 70004✓ 108
↓   SALES 60532 ·
2005 WAT   —   79L
2152 EUS   NR   14¼
2227 SMY   ·

45259 0210 CAR - CRWE

NOTE 70004
WORKED D705
BASING/WLOD ON 11/08

A notebook extract of that wonderful August weekend.

yet to arrive on the scene), notebook-carrying teenagers but most of us alighted at Basingstoke anyway, leaving them to look forward to their holiday in peace.

On Thursday, 18 August, and with another day's leave taken on the Friday, I headed north out of Euston on the 23.45 Barrow departure. With Preston and Chester visited during the morning, the 13.27 Manchester Victoria to Edinburgh was once again the chosen train into Scotland. I was not so fortunate on this occasion, with no banker provided up Shap and the Edinburgh portion being a pesky 'Splutterbug' DL – a series of ailing Black 5s conspired to deposit me at Edinburgh some forty-four minutes late. Heading for Kirkcaldy, this time without any regulation ticket complications, a much-appreciated Perth-allocated 44997 powered me over the Forth Bridge into Edinburgh. Neatly connecting into the 23.55 Birmingham departure, Brit 24 *Vulcan* took us the 141 miles from Carlisle to Crewe.

The rest of that Saturday was spent accumulating runs with ten different locomotives on WCML services – perhaps the biggest disappointment being

Stockport Edgeley-allocated Brit 70004 *William Shakespeare* was purposely diagrammed to work this 17.23 Southampton Docks departure on Tuesday, 16 August. This boat train, as arranged by enthusiasts in the Wimbledon divisional manager's office (DMO), was acting as a relief to the 17.30 Bournemouth departure and conveniently called at Basingstoke, enabling us enthusiasts to catch another run with her. She was returned to the LMR on a 'banana special' from Southampton Docks the following day.

letting Brit 48 go on the 10.47 Preston to Barrow, in the expectation of her returning on the 13.46 Barrow to Crewe. Sadly, she was failed at Barrow and replaced by Blackie 45014 – I never did get another chance of a run with her before her withdrawal at the year's end.

Rather than end up on the 01.00 Manchester on the Sunday morning, I took an unusual working that night, the 23.45 Preston to Liverpool Lime Street, and a 'required' Standard 5MT was in situ on the stock at 22.40. This earlier arrival into Wigan's unheated waiting room needed a great deal of stay-awake stamina and patience to avoid missing the 02.53 London train home. Boredom, mischievousness – call it what you like – but to pass the time and keep ourselves awake, the walls were graffitied with locomotive names and numbers, and fellow gricers' nicknames in the fashion of 'Kilroy was here' (a meme from the Second World War), accompanied by attempts at playing a piano that had been incongruously placed there. (During Covid lockdown, to pass the time one day by trawling through all my notebooks, I calculated that I had spent nearly four days of my life at this location waiting for trains.)

Tuesday, 23 August saw me make my final daytime visit to the GC line out of Marylebone and, although I was disappointed at the failure (hot box on the tender) of B1 61306, which had arrived that morning on the 08.15 ex-Nottingham and *was* going to work the 14.38 return, at least a compensatory 69 miles on the 16.38 train – Banbury's 9F 92228 maxing at 73½mph down Finmere Bank – was enjoyed. I made it as far north as the historic epicentre of the Great Central – Woodford Halse.

Having, on this final visit, travelled to the historic centre of the London extension of the GC, I stood surveying the scene while awaiting my returning train. Dereliction and abandonment would be the ideal descriptive words. The once-busy and extensive goods yard lay rusting away – it was a line in its death throes. Returning one final time on the 17.15 ex-Nottingham, I felt a sadness in witnessing another capitulation in the name of progress and by default, the continued erosion of my hobby.

With the ex-GC line closing in eight days' time, together with the fact that I had yet to travel the section north of Nottingham Victoria with steam, on Friday, 26 August, I caught the 18.10 Birkenhead departure out of Paddington to Banbury. This connected into the 19.15 Swindon to York service which, from Leicester Central, was the only passenger train booked for steam haulage over the speed-restricted section north of Nottingham – Tyseley's 44865 performing the honours.

Racing through Lancaster Castle on Saturday, 20 August, an unidentified Stanier 5MT heads a southbound train.

With Brit 48 having failed at Barrow, the 13.46 Barrow to Euston is seen departing Wigan North Western fifteen minutes late with Blackie 45014 later that day.

During that summer, the most commonly turned-out locomotive for the Preston Station pilot was Lostock Hall's Fairburn 42096, embellished with a chalked 73F (Ashford) allocation plate, referencing her eight-year sojourn at the Kent shed. She was withdrawn at the end of the year.

26TH AUGUST
16.38 SMY NR 1L
1702 VA — 2L
1810 PADD D1595 ✓
1932 BRN — 3L
21.16 BRN D7009 3L
L·GEN 44865
27TH AUGUST
0057 SH CEN — 6E
0200 SH MID 45676 6L
0252 NOR — 16L
0310 NUR 61022
↓ HML ←
0505 HB 45101
0528 HB 44962 7L
N 61019
0715 CC
0805 CC 44694 2L
0918 HB — 8L
0934 HB NR 6L
1038 PR. — 6L
1047 PR 70053 2L
1128 CAR — 2L
1202 CAR 45033 10L
1210 LC — 12L
1236 LC 44931
1308 PR. — 5E

1420
PRES * 44691 *9L (21)
1516 LL * ←
1557 LC 45227 9L (21)
1628 PRB — 5L
1745 PRES 44732 /
1817 WNW —
1915 WNW 70038 7L (6¼)
1939 PRES — 8L
2045 PRES 45449 10L (16¾)
21 VA. SA. — 8L.
2137 SA NR 2L (8¾)
2153 KTW — 2L
2217 KHW 44809 1L (8)
2230 PRES — 2L
2345 PRES 73131 2L (15¼)
0006 WNW — 3L
0253 WNW D1942 3ZL (35⅞)
↓ CR E312 - (158)
0620 EUS — 33L
0749 BF 55172 5L (15½)
0827 SMY — 3L

Another extract from my tattered notebooks, having survived all these years and later securely ensconced in the attaché case that always travelled with me.

Arriving at Sheffield Victoria at 00.51, it was just a few minutes' walk through the quiet city centre to connect into the six-locomotive Calder Valley mail train bash, after which I made my way to Preston. Following a dizzying day bombing up and down the WCML between Lancaster and Wigan, I ended up heading home via Wigan on the 23.45 Preston to Liverpool Lime Street, with yet another Patricroft Standard 5MT being red-lined.

There was no time the following week for a Basingstoke bash because, having booked three days' annual leave, I headed north on Tuesday, 30 August for the final weekend of the summer timetable that year. With the short-dated summer-only trains ceasing, the use of steam-powered passenger trains would, the following Monday, be severely curtailed.

Once more starting off on the Calder Valley circuit, because of the absence of the Saturday-only 08.05 Castleford to Blackpool train, I stayed aboard the B1 61019 *Nilghai*-powered 04.25 ex-Manchester through to York. Travelling over to Bradford with much walking between the Exchange and Forster Square Stations (fortunately, they were closer together than the present-day Interchange and Forster Square locations), at Bradford, of the seven ex-LMS tanks caught on portion workings, at least four were 'required'.

The 04.25 Manchester Victoria to York is seen at Normanton on Wednesday, 31 August. This train was worked there by a Newton Heath Black 5 and *anything* could be turned out by the Normanton foreman for the remaining 24 miles – on this occasion, it was York's 61019 *Nilghai*.

WAVY LINE WANDERINGS
STRANRAER, LLANDUDNO & DORSET

Perhaps an explanation as to the chapter heading is needed here. Regional printed timetables back in the 1960s were usually yearly publications. As such, train services that didn't run for the complete period of the publication had a wavy line inserted in the Timings column. This guided the reader to refer to the right side of the page where, together with any days shown at the column head (SX, FO, SO, etc.), the dates that the train was to run were shown. These trains, predominantly summer Saturdays-only, were anathema to Doctor Beeching, who accurately highlighted in his 1963 report that the cost of the maintenance of hundreds of coaching stock for use only during the summer months was uneconomical. Those very trains, however, because of their short-dated running, were often a rich source of steam locomotive provision and as such were homed in on by us chasers wherever they ran.

Okay, so back to that second night out (of an eventual five), and having headed to Manchester and caught the 01.00 Wigan departure – a surprise haulage by an Ivatt 3MT rather than the usual DSL – the shunt attachment at Wigan onto the rear of the 00.45 Liverpool to Scotland train was further enhanced by Brit 53 (rather than the usual Gateshead Peak DL) taking the ensemble onwards to Preston.

Fatigue was starting to catch up with me and, without the necessity to wake up at half-hourly intervals to pull the string on the time-operated wall heater, the weekend being the hottest of the month, in the minus-four-star waiting room, the next thing I knew, having missed the 05.35 Crewe stopper, was

Holyhead's Blackie 45247 rolling in at 07.00 on the 06.10 Blackpool South to Euston service. Taking her the short distance to Warrington, I headed off to the steam-saturated scene at Chester, visiting Shrewsbury and Birkenhead during the nine hours spent in the area. Although the mainstay power on the Welsh Marches trains was predominantly Black 5s, the variety that day was enhanced with two runs with Chester-allocated 76036 and 76044 on the Birkenhead section.

Following food replenishment at the all-night Crewe buffet and attempted sleep at Preston's waiting room, among the ten steam trains caught the following day over WCML metals between Wigan and Penrith, two were prized catches. Having arrived into Wigan NW behind a pristine ex-works Warrington Dallam Black 5MT (which wasn't to see the year out!) on the 05.35 ex-Preston, I was overjoyed to board what I thought was the 07.00 returning stopper to Preston with, by that date, a rare Springs Branch Stanier 2-6-4T – namely 30-year-old 42587. No one was more surprised than me when the train departed at 06.50. After enquiring from some other passengers, it turned out the train was a 06.48 unadvertised service for Leyland, there being sufficient patronage to run this and a 07.00 departure for workers at the massive British Motor Corporation (BMC) car plant there. Sure enough, having been turfed out at Leyland, the 07.00 service duly arrived with a mundane Black 5MT at its head to take me the short distance to Preston.

So, what was my other prized catch that day? LMR's final surviving Jubilee 45627 *Sierra Leone* – that's what! Having during that day journeyed to Manchester, Lancaster and Penrith, at 19.30 hours that evening I awaited, with bated breath, the arrival of the 19.00 Blackpool North to Liverpool Exchange train. There had been many rumours that summer of *Sierra Leone* being turned out by the Bank Hall foreman – all to no avail. *But* she had been reported heading to Blackpool that morning and we, there were a considerable number of us, were over the moon with ecstasy when she meandered into the former East Lancashire platforms at Preston in the fading light just after 19.30. What I didn't know until many years later was that volunteers from the Unofficial Volunteer Birkenhead Steam Cleaning Gang had cleaned her as this was to be her final run. She performed magnificently that evening, attaining 78mph through Maghull – only to be withdrawn just eight days later.

Liverpool Exchange Station, which was to witness Britain's final steam-hauled timetabled passenger train in August 1968, was opened in 1850 and was, in fact, a replacement for an earlier temporary structure just short of it

Standard 5MT 4-6-0 73073 calls at Chester General on Thursday, 1 September with the 07.40 Manchester Exchange to Llandudno. Commencing her life at Patricroft, this nomadic Crewe-built locomotive spent time on both the S&D and GC routes before returning to 9H in 1965. She was withdrawn in November 1967.

Later that same day at Birkenhead Woodside, the GWR Merseyside Terminus sees Stanier Tank 42647 awaiting departure with the 14.45 for Paddington, which she will work to Chester General. Recently transferred in from Springs Branch Wigan, this Birkenhead-allocated 2-6-4T was withdrawn upon the cessation of the Paddington services in the spring of 1967.

An unusually clean Aintree-allocated 45330 is caught passing Preston Station on Friday, 2 September. I finally snared her in August 1967 when, having been transferred to Warrington Dallam, she worked a Birmingham to Heysham train north of Crewe.

The LMR's sole remaining Jubilee, Bank Hall (Liverpool)-allocated 45627 *Sierra Leone*, is seen in the gathering gloom at Preston with the 19.00 Blackpool North to Liverpool Exchange service. There had been weeks of speculation within the enthusiast community whether she was to be turned out for a Preston portion or a Blackpool outing. She had been specifically cleaned by enthusiasts and was withdrawn eight days later.

in Great Howard Street. Jointly owned between the Lancashire & Yorkshire Railway (L&YR) and the East Lancashire Railway (ELR), the latter's insistence on calling it Tithebarn Street (its actual location) for the first nine years, until its absorption by the L&YR, no doubt caused confusion to any prospective customers. Damage to the overall glass roof during the Second World War was never fully repaired and by the time of my visits, the terminus had a somewhat abandoned feel about it. In 1969, all services excepting the Ormskirk and Southport EMUs and Wigan and Bolton DMUs were diverted to Lime Street. Six platforms were then sacrificed to enable tunnelling work in for the Merseyrail scheme which would allow services direct access via Moorfields to Liverpool Central. The final closure was enacted in April 1977.

After another night sharing the Preston waiting room with society's down and outs and following increasingly lengthy hours waiting for 'requirements' to materialise, I decided that I had rinsed the area of any further catches. I headed into Manchester that afternoon en route to Stockport Edgeley for the once-a-day Low Moor-resourced 19.35 for Bradford Exchange. Then, after a wonderful 45-mile ride through Pennines with a vociferous Fairburn 42116, I made my weary way home via Stalybridge, via Manchester and Wigan.

So ended my five-night, 109-hour marathon. What did I achieve? Statistically, the outing wasn't ground-breaking. A total mileage of 1,642, only 976 of which were steam, reaped forty-eight runs with forty-three different locomotives – only twenty-eight sating my needs. It could have been so much different – I might not have been so lucky – or it could have been better. Much as many enthusiasts would like to, you can't turn back the clock. I was grateful for what I did achieve. It was an unrepeatable scenario that is now written into the history books.

I had underused my SR season ticket over the summer months and with news of the impending arrival of six Type 4 Brush DLs, I planned that September to blitz the Bournemouth line steam services. Indeed, with the knowledge that the 17.30 Bournemouth departure was going over to DL and the 18.00 and 18.09 departures going to Class 33 DL and TC, the need was even more urgent. The result was my highest-ever monthly total steam mileage of over 4,900 miles. At least with the lengthy seamen's strike having ended, an additional choice of a returning train from Basingstoke was the 18.48 departure, namely the 16.00 Channel Islands boat train from Weymouth Quay to Waterloo.

As can be seen from the accompanying notebook extract, Saturday, 10 September saw me accumulate a wonderful 412 miles of Bulleid power over

Saturday, 3 September, and Kingmoor's 70016 *Ariel* is depicted arriving at Preston with a southbound parcel train. I finally caught up with her on the final week of regular all-year steam workings north of Crewe in March 1967.

A weary gricer, about to embark on the fifth overnight of his travels, takes one last photograph at Stockport Edgeley of Fairburn 42116 (with a Brummie mate in focus) awaiting departure with the 19.35 for Bradford Exchange. The train was to be dieselised eight weeks later.

a twelve-hour period. This seemingly crazy way of spending a day was, in my mind, justified by the fact that by this time next year it would all be history.

On Tuesday 13th, Nine Elms Driver West attained 92mph with 'The Pram' (35023) on the Salisbury run. Quite a few of the drivers at this south London depot were entering into the spirit of the closing days of steam and were thrashing the locomotives, using the logic that they were all destined for the cutter's torch so whatever damage might be caused by over-enthusiastic driving would not be noticed.

Scotland was on the agenda on the mid-month weekend, principally, if my memory serves me correctly, to try to catch runs with steam on the Glasgow to Gourock lines – news that they were to be dieselised in the near future was being circulated. 'The Northern Irishman' to Stranraer that night wonderfully produced Brit 9 *Alfred the Great*, piloted from Ayr with 45423. The pyrotechnics produced by both locomotives south of Ayr were pleasingly cherished in the darkness of a pre-dawn morning.

After calling in at Kilmarnock in the thwarted hope to travel with one of Hurlford's 77xxxs, the original objective, having then headed on to Glasgow, was also unfulfilled in that all the non-rush-hour services along the Clyde coast were DMUs. Just after noon, however, Standard 5MT 73079 was noted, propelling in a rake of non-corridor stock. Dashing round to the platform, I jumped aboard, not knowing or caring where it was going.

It turned out to be a 12.18 'Race Special' to Ayr and I experienced a much-appreciated 40 miles there. Back into Glasgow and with a complete absence of steam, I admitted defeat and headed south to Carlisle for the guaranteed 20.25 Perth departure, which was taken to Carstairs with Brit 5 *John Milton*. With an arrival time of 22.02 at Carstairs, together with the then punitive opening hours of the adjacent pub meaning it *should* stop serving at 22.00, the landlord took pity on us and stated that in future if we phoned up from Carlisle, he would have several pints on the bar waiting for us. We had to take into consideration that if we were to continue on the Perth train to Coatbridge then we had just thirty minutes or so prior to the train's recommencement of its journey to quaff as many of the beers as possible – access to the pub was via the back door of course!

On this particular Saturday morning, however, we returned to Carlisle and having had some food replenishment at the staff canteen (a wag having chalked near the entrance that due to increased patronage from us chasers prices would be reduced – some hope), Brit 29 *Shooting Star* was taken for the 141 miles to

Bournemouth-allocated 35013 *Blue Funnel* on Saturday, 10 September with the 13.30 Weymouth departure. She was to become one of the final Merchants at Nine Elms, thus enabling me to attain 1,748 miles with her.

10th September 1966

0733 SMY   NR   ✓   (14¾)
0800 VA   —   1L
0835 WAT. 34077 1L   (79¼)
1038 SOT. —   12L
1126 SOT   35008 6L   (79¼)
1303 WAT   —   3L
1330 WAT   35013 ✓   (47¾)
1433 BAS   —   1L
1505 BAS   34032 2E   (47¾)
1609 WAT   —   8L
1635 WAT   35014 1L   (79¼)
1819 SOT   —   3L
1832 SOT   34009 2L   (79¼)
2030 WAT   —   5E
2041 E+C   NR   ✓   (3)
2049 HRN   —   1E
2050 HRN   5174 MR 1L   (6¾)
2107 BP   —   1E
2108 BP   NR.   1L   (4)
2113 SMY   —

                Blue 2 HAP
                6006

A notebook extract depicting my three exits and entrances within twelve hours at Waterloo!

Crewe on the Edinburgh to Birmingham 02.08 departure. After spending the day on the Welsh Marches services (five Black 5s, one 76xxx and a Fairburn tank), two more of Stanier's finest were caught in the Preston area before heading home on the inevitable 02.53 Wigan to Euston.

The remainder of the month, with Jim Reeves' 'Distant Drums' monopolising the airwaves, was spent on SR metals. Evening commutes, days off and two overnights contributed to that month's high steam mileage – the one solitary 'requirement' being 80015 on the evening 'Kenny Belle' on Monday, 19 September.

On the 26th, having travelled down to Southampton in the morning and having spent the day bombing up and down between there and Basingstoke, I was to be found boarding the lightweight 18.38 Waterloo departure from Salisbury. Driver De'arth, working it to his home depot of Basingstoke, certainly gave *Okehampton* some welly that night, passing Grateley at 75½mph before maxing at 94mph at Red Posts Junction prior to the necessary hard braking for the Andover stop. Not content with that, he maxed at 90mph between Overton and Oakley stations before adverse signals from Worting Junction slowed his progress.

Prioritising unmodifieds and Merchants, my mileages behind any particular locomotive were carefully monitored. The rivalry among fellow enthusiasts was to try to obtain at least 1,000 miles behind as many as possible. One such example being Merchant 8 *Orient Line*, with 630 miles covered within seventy-two hours, as can be seen in the accompanying notebook extract (see page 129).

Allocated to Crewe Works, the last surviving 0-6-0 ex-LMS Fowler-designed 4F, 38-year-old 44525 shuffles around the station on Saturday, 17 September, just days before withdrawal.

'Borrowed' power for the 08.35 Waterloo to Weymouth on Monday, 19 September was Colwick-allocated Blackie 45222, a regular on GC line trains, seen here arriving into Southampton Central.

BR Mogul 76033 is at Southampton Central with the 10.43 for Bournemouth Central. This 12-year-old had arrived on the SR at Brighton from the ER and was Guildford-allocated at the time of this shot.

That September was the last month before many steam workings were taken over by an influx of Class 47s together with Class 33/TC units coming on stream, so, making the fullest usage of my season ticket, I accumulated over 4,900 steam miles. As part of that bash, 34057 *Biggin Hill* (with the infamous Driver Porter) is seen at Southampton Central on Monday, 26 September with the 08.35 Waterloo to Weymouth.

At Waterloo we see the 15.30 for Weymouth on Wednesday, 28 September with Bournemouth's Merchant 35008 *Orient Line* at the head. About to embark on a mileage-bashing trip, I was to accumulate over 630 miles with her during the following three days, leading to a total of 1,450 miles before her withdrawal from Nine Elms in July 1967.

Documentary proof of
my *Orient Line* chase.

Having travelled with *Orient Line* to Weymouth and back on the up-mails overnight, the following morning, Thursday, 29 September, sees Exmouth Junction refugee 34108 *Wincanton* taking water at Southampton Central while working the 08.35 Waterloo to Weymouth.

```
28th September
1530 WAT  x 35008      /
P9 26 WEY    —       2E
2213 WEY  x 35008    ✓
  ↓   Bomo 35008
0411 WAT    —        /
0530 WAT  34009      ✓
0644 BAS    —       5L
0705 BAS  73087      -
1522 WAT    —       5L
0835 WAT  34108      ✓
1038 SOR    —      10L
11 16 SOT 34037    14L
1303 WAT    —      12L
1330 WAT  34100
1431 BAS    —       4L
1505 BAS  73016    2L
1609 WAT    —       3E
1635 WAT. 35008
18 19 SOT   —        ✓
1818 SOT  34036    7L
2025 WAT    —       2L
2214 BF   NR      15L
2257 Smy    —
```

A notebook extract of the previously referred to overnight bash on the Southern.

AUTUMN OUTINGS
LYMINGTON, GOOLE & BRADFORD

Having arrived into Waterloo on the up TPO on the morning of Saturday, 1 October, a pleasant surprise was my final 'required' SR-allocated, double-chimneyed 75xxx, namely 75075, on the 04.40 Salisbury departure – this was itself unusual, i.e. a steam-hauled passenger train with a booked stop at Vauxhall. Venturing back into Hampshire I was happy to red-line two examples of those aesthetically pleasing Standard 4MT tanks, 80016 on an Eastleigh local and sister 80019 on the Lymington branch, which were much valued.

The 5½-mile-long line from Brockenhurst to Lymington Town was opened in 1858, absorbed by the L&SWR in 1860 and extended to the Pier Station, thus connecting to the Isle of Wight ferries to Yarmouth, in 1884. For many years, the branch trains were worked in push–pull mode by Drummond M7s, the through-trains from London having ceased in the early 1960s. During 1966, and indeed until DEMUs displaced them in April 1967, I always readied myself upon arriving into Brockenhurst to alight speedily if a 'required' tank was working the connecting branch trains that day. This 'alertness' saw me acquire runs with all the remaining stud of Bournemouth's BR Standard 4MTs and Ivatt 3MTs. Indeed, on one cold frosty Sunday in January 1967, much to the guard's amazement, I made two consecutive return trips – the Sunday afternoon changeover (light engine to and from 70F) of Ivatts, reaping runs with two more. Although the juice rail was activated in January 1967, due to a quirk within the promotion, transfer and redundancy (PT&R) arrangements regarding the steam drivers' redundancy packages, the services remained steam worked until that April.

Indeed, the numbers of 'required' SR-allocated locomotives that I needed were falling fast, resulting from a combination of withdrawals and alert observations by myself when passing through locations such as Eastleigh, Southampton, Brockenhurst and Bournemouth.

I wasn't completely ignoring the other regions though, and Friday, 7 October saw me head out of St Pancras to connect into Saturday's 02.00 Sheffield Midland to Leeds City, with the train now the preserve of a Peak DL since the winter timetable had kicked in. Alighting at Normanton, at least the Calder Valley trains still provided some entertainment – the 04.25 ex-Manchester Victoria was taken forward from Normanton into York by one of 55E's two Fairburns, namely 42149. Along with a gathering of other southern haulage-bashers, I was in the area to travel on the 'Crab Commemorative Rail Tour', which was worked from Wakefield Kirkgate to Goole by a pristine WD 2-8-0, returning with one of the few remaining Hughes Crab 2-6-0s – both representatives of classes I had never travelled with.

Goole was reached in 1848 by the L&YR from Knottingley and its station in the docks was superseded by the current one, which was opened by the North Eastern Railway in 1869 upon extending the line through to Hull. During the hour or so we had at Goole we were allowed to wander around the shed, which was conveniently adjacent to the station. After reboarding the train we alighted at Wakefield Kirkgate at 17.40 and went to Westgate Station to catch Bolton's 44927 into Bradford Exchange (which had become a shed by that date, void of passenger work). We then caught the 22.00 from there to Huddersfield with an ailing B1 *Nyala* (she struggled with the one BSK up the incline to Bowling Junction), changing onto the York TPO and finally the omnipresent 01.00 to Wigan and home. All in all, a very sound outing.

Another Saturday and another rail tour. On Saturday, 15 October, on the privately sponsored 'Steam Again to the West Country' rail tour, with all profits going to the Woking Homes orphanage, I attained my first ton (100mph-plus speed). Driver Hooker (70A), who had deliberately engineered a duty exchange to work the tour, reached 102mph down Andover Bank. The locomotive, the ever-reliable 'Pram', handed over the train at Westbury to sister Merchant 26 *Lamport & Holt Line* and although a request for a seventy-five-minute schedule to Exeter was rejected by the WR authorities, the eventual ninety-one-minute one was bettered by – you've guessed it – sixteen minutes! Merchant 26 was in good nick that day, attaining 88mph approaching Templecombe with her eight-vehicle load. And the high speeds hadn't finished. Merchant 23 took

The cleanest WD 2-8-0 I ever witnessed was this one at Goole on Saturday, 8 October. Wakefield's 90076 had worked the 32-mile leg of the 'Crab Commemorative Rail Tour' from Wakefield itself.

Birkenhead's 'Crab' 2-6-0 42942 is a long way from home at Goole, preparing to return the tour train back to Liverpool. This 34-year-old was destined to become the last of her class – her withdrawal coming in January 1967.

Weymouth's Merchant 35007 on Tuesday, 11 October with the 18.30 Weymouth departure. She was withdrawn from Nine Elms at the very end of SR steam in July 1967 – with my personal mileage with her at 2,003.

The 18.09 commuter departure for Basingstoke with a very dirty Eastleigh-allocated 34023 *Blackmore Vale* the same evening. Although officially not withdrawn until the end in July 1967, she was not used for several weeks beforehand to avoid damage prior to a lifetime in preservation.

over the train again at Salisbury and passed Brookwood at 91mph. It was an exhilarating day out and a credit to all concerned.

The weather went a bit crazy after that, dropping from 26°C on that day to a wind-chilling 9°C four days later, before returning to the normality of the low twenties a few days after. I have to admit, I rarely documented the weather – my hobby was imbibed upon irrespective of conditions!

During the following week, in which the iconic Ford Cortina Mark II was launched, Merchant 26, obviously still in fine fettle, was pushed to 88½mph on the lightweight Salisbury route by Gaffney of 70A. The 17.30 ex-Waterloo, although booked for a Brush DL, was now, more often than not, a steam replacement because of the DLs' unreliability. Following several late starts causing rush-hour delays to a considerable number of services, it reverted to steam haulage from the 14th of the following month. There's progress for you!

On 21 October, the Aberfan disaster occurred when a collapsing coal mine spoil heap engulfed the local school resulting in 144 deaths. Music

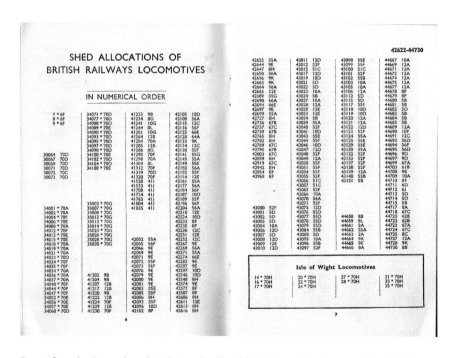

Extract from the December-dated *Locoshed* book highlighting the absence of any WR entries together with the decreasing number of Bulleids and LMS tanks.

wise, The Four Tops' 'Reach Out I'll Be There' topped the charts for three weeks that month.

The early hours of Saturday, 22 October saw me, having taken the 23.45 Barrow departure out of Euston, aboard the 05.35 Preston to Crewe en route to Chester and another steam-saturated day on the Welsh Marches trains. The Chester foreman was adept at 'borrowing' visiting locomotives from other depots and to this end, a Stourton (Leeds) Blackie was turned out for the 09.33 to Shrewsbury. All one had to do was stand at the western end of Chester Station and await whatever was being turned out for the reversal of the Paddington to Birkenhead trains. Fellow trainspotters, i.e., those *not* bothered about being hauled by any particular locomotive, were always willing to offer up information on what had occurred prior to my arrival and by relying on their observations, one could sometimes predict which trains would have returning locomotives from either Shrewsbury or Birkenhead.

By about 15.00, having, in my opinion, rinsed the area of 'requirements', I made for Warrington to intercept the Brit-worked to Crewe, 13.46 Barrow to Euston, before making my way to Stockport for a second 45-mile run over the Pennines to Bradford on the all-stations (if requested!) stopper. Then, as two weeks previously, I took the 22.00 from there via Huddersfield, Stalybridge and Manchester to home, arriving into Euston an hour earlier than usual, at 05.16, because of the clock change.

The final catch of the month, on Saturday 29th, was Standard Mogul 76009. I travelled with her the 8 miles from Hamworthy Junction to Bournemouth Central having earlier that outing caught *Port Line* to the south coast resort aboard the prestigious 'Bournemouth Belle'.

NOVEMBER

RAIL TOURS GALORE
STRATFORD, BACUP & WEYMOUTH

The month started off well on Tuesday 1st, with a 'required' 80012 working the 17.20 Clapham Junction and 17.36 return trains. As the outward train was empty coaching stock (ECS), permission had to be granted by the guard should anything happen en route – the production of the ever-present BR identity card usually satisfying officialdom.

A North West visit on 4–6 November produced a disappointing mere three 'requirements' out of the ten locomotives I caught. By default, although I was unaware of it at the time, only finding out several months later courtesy of a printed publication, it was the final steam working of the 15.20 Bradford to Stockport and 19.30 return, with Low Moor's regular Fairburn 42116 doing the honours.

This train was a leftover from a once-through service between Bradford and London Euston. The northbound one was shown in the timetable as having request stops at most stations 'upon notice given to the guard upon departing Stockport'. It was Bonfire Night that evening and the feisty tank certainly contributed her show of pyrotechnics when battling the gradients en route. Another last journey I made that night was on my homeward train, the 22.00 Bradford to Huddersfield, which was to disappear in a January 1967 timetable change with no passenger vehicles being conveyed on it after that date.

Following several unexceptional Basingstoke visits during the week, on Saturday, 12 November, I embarked upon 'The Shakespearian Rail Tour', enticed by the use of the privately owned 4-6-0 *Clun Castle* and a Pannier tank visit to Stourbridge Town. Starting out of Waterloo, Driver Porter of Nine

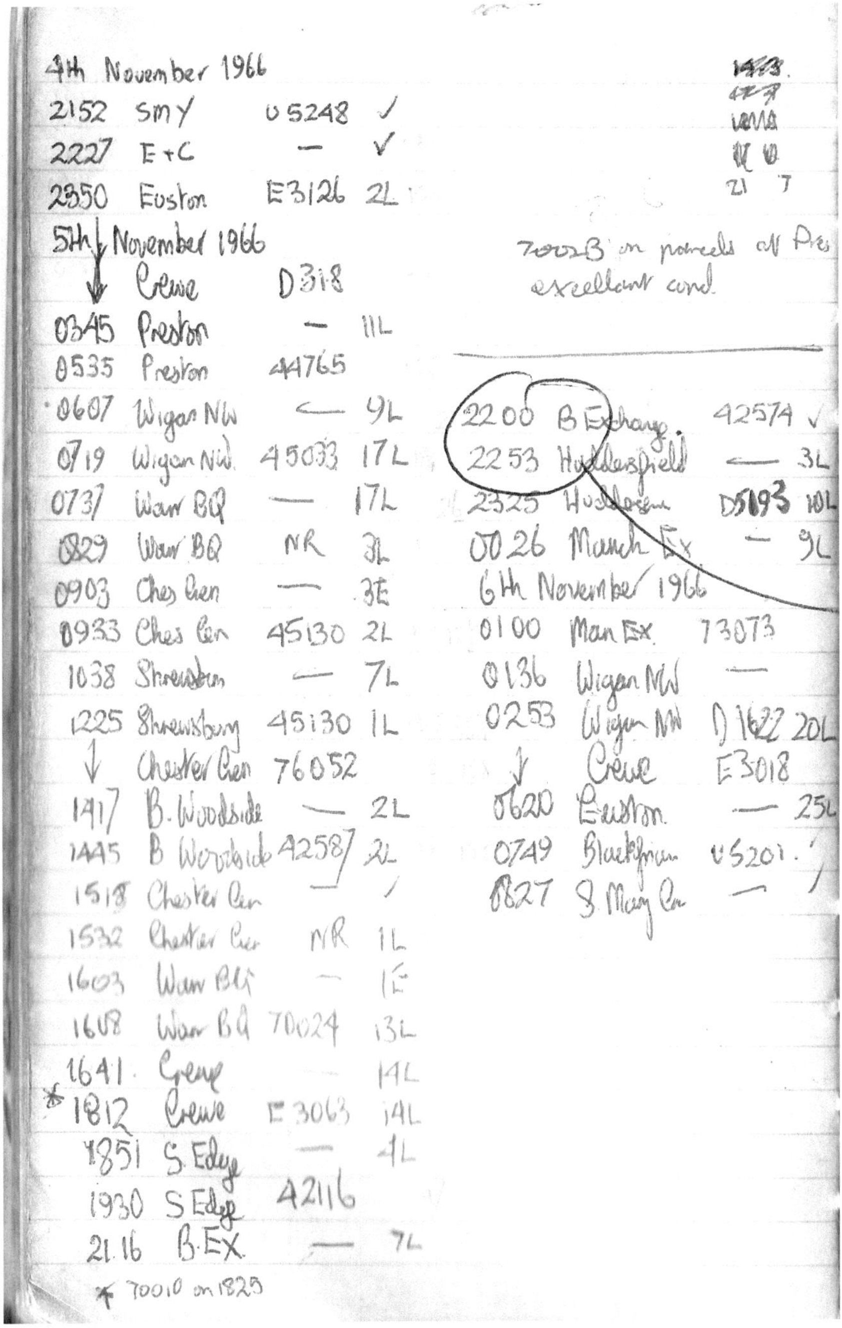

4th November 1966
2152 SmY   U5248 ✓
2227 E+C   — ✓
2350 Euston   E3126 2L

5th November 1966
↓ Crewe   D318
0345 Preston   — 11L
0535 Preston   44765
0607 Wigan NW   ← 9L
0719 Wigan NW   45033 17L
0737 Waw BQ   — 17L
0829 Waw BQ   NR 3L
0903 Ches Gen   — 3E
0933 Ches Gen   45130 2L
1038 Shrewsbury   — 7L
1225 Shrewsbury   45130 1L
↓ Chester Gen 76052
1417 B. Woodside   — 2L
1445 B Woodside 42587 2L
1518 Chester Gen   ✓
1532 Chester Gen   NR 1L
1603 Waw BQ   — 1E
1608 Waw BQ 70024 13L
* 1641 Crewe   — 14L
* 1812 Crewe   E3063 14L
1851 S. Edge   — 4L
1930 S Edge 42116
21.16 B.EX   — 7L
* 70010 on 1823

7002B on parcels at Pres
excellent cond.

2200 B Exchange   42574 ✓
2253 Huddersfield   ← 3L
2325 Huddersm   D5193 10L
0026 Manch Ex   — 9L
6th November 1966
0100 Man Ex   73073
0136 Wigan NW   —
0253 Wigan NW   D1622 20L
↓ Crewe   E3018
0620 Euston   — 25L
0749 Blackfriars   U5201 ✓
0827 S Mary Gn   — ✓

A notebook extract detailing the first weekend of November's outing.

Elms (who else?) gave the tour a flying start by taking Unmodified *Exmouth* (the requested *Lapford* having been failed earlier that week) up to a seat-grabbing 75mph through Bracknell.

From Reading, 'The Pram' took us to Banbury where a rather down-at-heel-looking *Clun Castle* took over to Stratford-upon-Avon. Appropriately, Brit 4 *William Shakespeare*, albeit with a collapsed brick-arch, then took the train to Stourbridge Junction where, disappointingly, the planned Pannier visit to Stourbridge Town was supplanted by a DMU, there being no fit GWR tanks available.

The proposed return route via Dudley and Swan Village was declined by the LMR authorities at the last minute, citing locomotive route restrictions and track condition, causing us to travel as per outward, via Rowley Regis. After having been banked out of Snow Hill Station, *Clun Castle* achieved 74mph down Hatton Bank before being supplanted at Banbury with Merchant 23. Although a further delay at Old Oak Common awaiting a pilotman resulted in a fifty-five-minute-late arrival into London's Victoria Station, my earlier than normal return home somewhat surprised my parents, who were more often used to hearing the key being turned in the door in either the early hours or anytime on a Sunday.

Another day, another rail tour. 'The West Country Special' on 13 November turned out to be the very last steam train that the WR authorities permitted over their Great Western Main Line (GWML) metals. Starting out of Victoria, Standard 73065 (rather than the requested green-liveried 73029) took a convoluted route via Redhill to Westbury, handing over to Unmodified Bulleid *Bideford*. She was well up to the task and, having taken us down the GWML to Exeter, she took the 50 miles on undulating gradients up the switchback ex-L&SWR line to Yeovil in just forty-nine minutes, maxing at 86½mph east of Crewkerne.

On one evening that month, when I arrived into Basingstoke on my regular commute, the London-bound 'Bournemouth Belle' stood engineless in the platform. She eventually departed at 18.47 (due into Waterloo at 18.59!) with a Standard 5MT, which had been hastily prepared at the nearby sub-shed of Eastleigh. Perhaps the occupants were given an extra glass of wine as compensation.

Moving on to 23 November and Nine Elms were obviously short of power that night because all they could turn out for the eleven-vehicle, heavily laden 18.09 Basingstoke train was Standard 4MT 76064. With a maximum of 50mph through Berrylands, she took forty-eight minutes to get to Woking, where she

This is Ascot, and the 'Shakespearian Rail Tour' on Saturday, 12 November calls for a photo shoot with Salisbury's 34015 *Exmouth*.

I was on this tour mainly to obtain a run with the recently preserved 7029 *Clun Castle*, seen here at Banbury preparing to take the train forward the 35 miles to Stratford-upon-Avon.

With the promised two 57xx pannier tanks unavailable to take the tour down the branch, the replacement DMU is seen at Stourbridge Town.

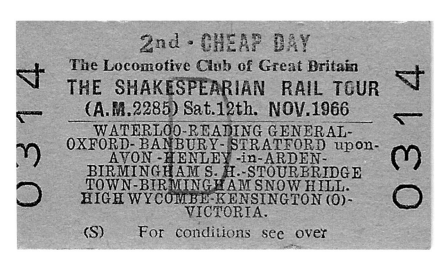

The ticket for the tour.

Standard 5MT 73065, standing in for the requested green-liveried 73029, is seen calling at Norwood Junction for water on Sunday, 13 November with an unusually routed Victoria to the West of England rail tour.

With the Standard having brought the 'West Country Special Tour' from Victoria, Light Pacific 34019 *Bideford* is at Westbury about to work the 127 miles via Exeter to Salisbury.

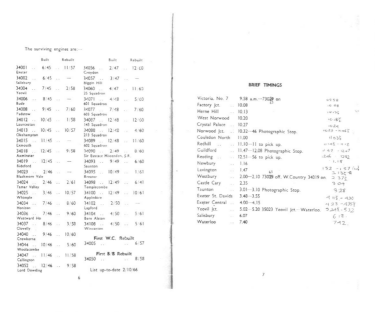

An extract from the accompanying brochure.

eventually departed twenty-two minutes late, having raised enough steam to continue. In the meantime, several irate bowler-hatted commuters came up the platform at Woking to complain to the driver, fireman and anyone else wearing a railway uniform. No doubt they were looking forward to the electrification the following year.

The final rail tour undertaken that month was 'The Three Counties Special', which ran on Saturday, 26 November. Having already commenced the visit on a high, with a 'required' Brit on the 06.10 ex-Blackpool South and a rare Carnforth beast on the Belfast express train into Manchester, there was sufficient time at Victoria's Travellers Fare buffet for something to eat prior to the tour's departure time of 10.00. And what a tour!

Consisting of just four ex-LMS vehicles, a Stanier tank took us over what is now the East Lancashire Railway metals to Bacup before returning to Bury for two elderly Jinties to take us the 22 miles to Stockport where, following another change of tank locomotive, this time an Ivatt, we departed for Buxton. A rare haulage by a J94 saddle tank then took us to Millers Dale (with the Mickey on the rear due to braking incompatibility) before taking a circuitous route into the doomed Manchester Central.

I could have made my way home then but, as ever, the greed for possible new haulages kicked in and having forfeited a night in my comfortable bed, it was well worth it with a further two Stanier 5MTs being scratched.

The typical Manchester weather of drizzling rain and fog, which persisted throughout the day, can be seen here at Bacup, where Trafford Park's 42644 (withdrawn the following March) was running round the 'Three Counties Rail Tour' on Saturday, 26 November. Bacup was to lose its passenger services a week later.

Forty-year-old Vulcan Foundry-built and Fowler-designed 3F 47383 is, together with 47202, at Bury about to take the tour forward the 22 miles to Stockport. This Newton Heath locomotive, although withdrawn just weeks later, was reinstated for eight months at Westhouses. She has survived into preservation at the Severn Valley Railway.

Sister Jinty, 67-year-old 47202, fitted with condensation equipment for tunnel working in London, was not so lucky, her withdrawal at Newton Heath coming that December.

British Railways Board (M)

Manchester Rail Travel Society
" THREE COUNTIES SPECIAL "
SATURDAY, 12th NOVEMBER, 1966

Manchester (Victoria), Oldham, Rochdale,
Bury, Bacup, Bury, Clifton Jct.,
Manchester (Victoria), Stockport
(Edgeley), Disley, Buxton, Millersdale,
Chinley, Manchester (Central)

SECOND CLASS   For conditions see over

0218   0218

The ticket for the tour is dated for 12 November, but it was put back two weeks for 'operational purposes'.

```
25th November                              43/4
  2152   Smy    v5216   2L        ** DIVERTED VIA
  2227   E+C     —      2L        ACTON GRANGE JCN
  2350   EUS    E3169   2L        FRODSHAM JCN
  26th November                   WEAVER JCN
    ↓     CREW   D1622
  0345   PRES     —     15L
  0555   PRES    NR.     ✓        2345 PRESTON (✓) 45187
  0607   K+W      —      1E       00.06 WIGAN NW (L) —
  0640   K+W    7005)    ✓        0253 WIGAN NW (2L) D1622
  0652   PRES     —      2L       {        CREWE      E317
  0714   PRES   45373   10L       0620 EUSTON (54L)
  0808   MAN.V.   —     12L       0747  BF    v5009
  42644  MAN(vic) - BURY          0857  Smy
  47202 }
  47383 } BURY - STOCKPORT
  41204  STOCKPORT - BUXTON
  68006                                70010 m 2145 Crewe
 ⌐41204 } BUXTON - MANCHESTER
 └68006 }              MILLERS DALE
  41204  MILLERS DALE - MANCHESTER
  1705   M(OR)    NR     1L
  1806   CREWE    —      ✓
  1825   CREWE  7005).   9L
  1939   PRESTON  —      6L
  2045   PRESTON 45005  12L
  2114   ST ANNES  —    17L
  2137   ST ANNES NR
  2206   PRESTON   —
```

A notebook extract depicting services caught before and after the tank tour.

THE SOUTHERN SOJOURN
SHANKLIN, KENSINGTON & HAMPSHIRE

The year finished as it started – on Southern metals. Taking into consideration the fact that the 17.41 Salisbury departure out of Waterloo had gone Warship-hauled (until January 1967, when it was to go EMU) and the 18.09 was going Class 33+TC sometime that December, along with the returning 15.50 ex-Weymouth (20.25 arrival) going Class 33+TC, I spent the entire month getting the most out of my season ticket on the fast-dwindling Waterloo steam services. For sure, it was the appropriately titled 'Green, Green Grass of Home', sung by Tom Jones, which we had to listen to for seven whole weeks!

On a brighter note, now that I was working at Wimbledon, on my daily commute from Kent I could, subject to 'right-time' running, travel on the morning 'Kenny Belle' on the way to work. Whenever a main-line driver recognised me on the train, he usually made a special effort to storm along with the four-vehicle train. On one occasion, he reached a heady 51mph approaching Latchmere Junction on the returning 08.33 ex-Kensington. I was the sole passenger. An added bonus was often seeing some of the London Transport pannier tanks at work in the Lille Bridge area. To this end, on Tuesday, 6 December, my final 'required' Nine Elms Standard 4MT 80154 was scratched.

That same evening, the Warship DL for the 17.41 ran short of fuel and was dispatched to Stewarts Lane, so I enjoyed 47¾ miles with the wonderful substitution Light Pacific 34019 *Bideford*. The same thing happened the following night, with the same unmodified, as the Warship DL *fortuitously* failed again on its inward journey. This was a strange diagram as the DL from the 17.41 took forward the 19.00 Waterloo to Exeter from Salisbury – itself steam-worked from Waterloo.

On Saturday, 10 December, always keeping an eye on the New Forest stopping services in order to travel with all the SR steam locomotives, I espied Mogul 76066 at Eastleigh while haring through with *Blue Funnel* on the 10.30 Waterloo. I backtracked upon arrival into Bournemouth Central to catch her for the 1¾ miles in from Pokesdown. I took a visit to the adjacent Bournemouth shed – without being turfed out – to see eleven locos in steam and another five which were dead. Walking among these sleeping leviathans at rest and viewing them from ground level was awe inspiring, and I still, to this day, admire those who tamed them and harnessed their power even though the run-down and filthy condition of them was visible for all to see.

Returning that evening on the 15.50 ex-Weymouth and 'Sir Useless Missenden' suffered a forty-minute delay at Basingstoke with only 16½ vacuum brake available – no odds, though, with 78mph maximum en route to London.

A very derelict-looking Standard, Bournemouth's 76009 awaits departure on Saturday, 10 December with the 13.52 stopper for Southampton Central.

On Wednesday, 14 December, none of the six Brush DLs were working. Although it must have been the shed foreman's nightmare to conjure up replacement steam locomotives together with crews at short notice, it was sheer heaven to us steam chasers.

Friday, 16 December saw me embark on the first of four overnights that month, starting with 'The Pram' on the 'Bournemouth Belle'. Driver Porter was on the 20.51 arrival that evening and although promising a ton, he managed 94mph with *Clan Line*, blaming the bad fire left by the Weymouth men on arrival at Bournemouth Central.

After arriving into Waterloo, to occupy the night hours prior to my visit to the Isle of Wight steam scene, I travelled westward to Brockenhurst, returning to Basingstoke on the London-bound TPO. Departing from there behind *Lapford* on the 02.30 Waterloo to Portsmouth Harbour, and accompanying fellow enthusiast Squire (nicknamed due to his dapper appearance including a bow tie), we crossed the Solent for a final bash on the Isle of Wight – steam services were ceasing there on the 31st, with the line closing for electrification work to progress. This archaic system would surely have been a tourist magnet had somebody (with money) had the foresight to purchase the infrastructure and run it as a preserved railway – the section that has survived and is flourishing being an example. Fortune shone upon me that day, with three out of the four of these ancient tanks in circulation – *Shanklin*, *Calbourne* and *Merstone* – being 'required'. Having breakfasted at a café on the Shanklin seafront, I recrossed the Solent and returned to the main-line steam scene at Southampton for the remainder of that day.

On Wednesday, 21 December, Nine Elms Driver Evans, whose claim to fame was driving the final steam locomotive out of Waterloo (Merchant 30 on 7 July, en route to Nine Elms shed), thrashed *Biggin Hill* on the lightweight Salisbury run and attained 84mph through Esher and 64mph between Clapham Junction and Waterloo, taking a mere five minutes and twenty-two seconds between the latter two locations. Fast approach or what?

Following a shortage of fit steam locomotives combined with the Brush DLs' unreliability and extra Christmas parcels traffic, eight previously withdrawn steam locomotives were returned to service. One of them, 34032 *Camelford*, worked the 18.38 Salisbury to Waterloo on Thursday the 22nd.

The up TPO, 22.13 Weymouth to Waterloo, had now gone over to Brush DL haulage and so a common 'move' among us was to alight at Woking at its 03.03 arrival to connect into either the 02.30 Waterloo to Portsmouth or the

MN 35023 *Holland-Afrika Line* (for reasons unknown, nicknamed 'The Pram'!) arrives at Southampton Central on Saturday, 24 December with the 11.18 Weymouth to Waterloo.

Ex-WR, now Guildford-allocated, Standard 5MT 73092 is at Southampton Central that Christmas Eve, having arrived with a 12.25 'Shoppers' Special' from Bournemouth Central.

02.45 Waterloo to Bournemouth Central. If the latter was taken, you could get as far west as Wareham and then return to London on 'The Royal Wessex'. Perhaps the reader can now appreciate how my steam mileage was so high that particularly cold year.

The final Friday of that month saw a 'required' Standard 3MT 82029 being caught on the morning 'Kenny Belle' before I completed a day's work at Wimbledon and then pushed my mileage with Merchant 23 over the magic 1,000 miles – the first of an eventual 15 – on that evening's 18.30 out of Waterloo.

On the following day, after another overnight, a dishevelled enthusiast treated himself to an out-and-back trip on 'The Bournemouth Belle', with *Saunton* on the way down and *Callington* coming back. I wonder what the attendants thought of this youth, albeit still wearing a tie (although perhaps at an unusual angle), producing a valid ticket on this pristine service!

So that's it, folks. At the beginning of 1966 there were 2,987 steam locomotives on BR's books, and by the year's end the numbers were down to 1,689. It was a sad, sorry sight – everywhere steam was being dispensed with, no matter how young and fit they were: sacrificed in the name of modernisation. I hope you enjoyed my journeys.

None of us knew back then the plethora of steam locomotives that were to be saved from the cutter's torch throughout the UK mainland. Having initially been staring into the abyss of despair, what a wonderful steam scene we have these days – on both main-line and preserved railways. Well done to all involved in the resurrection and running of the 300-plus examples we have with us.

APPENDIX

Miles Travelled, 1966

1966	Steam Miles	EL/EMU Miles*	DL/ DMU Miles	Total Miles	Days Out	Nights Out
Jan	626	--	--	626	9	--
Feb	1558	75	143	1776	16	1
Mar	3077	257	262	3596	21	3
Apr	3563	67	378	4008	20	2
May	2407	231	908	3546	21	5
Jun	2661	507	915	4083	21	5
Jul	3253	862	1721	5836	19	10
Aug	3585	948	1357	5890	17	12
Sep	4923	474	837	6234	23	7
Oct	2667	499	457	3623	21	4
Nov	2736	688	260	3684	21	4
Dec	4165	64	306	4535	23	4
Total	35221	4672	7544	47437	232	57

★ Excluding my EMU commute from Kent to London/Wimbledon.

Waterloo Departures and Arrivals, 1966

Dep.	To	Inst.		Arri.	From	Inst.
03.15	Southampton	1		04.11	22.13 ex-Weymouth[4]	4
04.40	Salisbury	1		08.22	07.05 ex-Basingstoke	2
05.30	Bournemouth	3		11.02	07.30 ex-Weymouth[3]	3
08.30	Weymouth	3		13.03	09.21 ex-Weymouth	2
08.35	Weymouth	6		14.16	11.07 ex-Bournemouth	3
09.30	Bournemouth	2		16.09	12.59 ex-Bournemouth	5
10.30	Weymouth	4		16.52	13.25 ex-Weymouth	3
11.30	Bournemouth	4		18.39	15.08 ex-Bournemouth	7
12.30	Bournemouth[1]	6		18.53	16.37 ex-Bournemouth[1]	1
13.30	Weymouth	6		19.45	16.00 ex-Weymouth[5]	12
15.30	Weymouth	2		20.25	15.50 ex-Weymouth	46
16.35	Weymouth[3]	5		20.29	18.35 ex-Salisbury[2]	73
17.00	Exeter	1		20.51	17.30 ex-Weymouth	12
17.09	Basingstoke	32			Railtours	6
17.23	Bournemouth	1				
17.30	Bournemouth	40				
17.41	Basingstoke	26				
18.00	Salisbury	24				
18.09	Basingstoke	4				
18.30	Weymouth	1				
18.54	Basingstoke	3				
21.20	Bournemouth	3				
22.35	Weymouth[4]	2				
	Railtours	6				
	Total	**186**			**Total**	**185**

1 'Bournemouth Belle'.
2 Retimed 18.38 ex-Salisbury; arri. 20.36 from May.
3 'The Royal Wessex'.
4 Travelling Post Office.
5 Channel Isles boat train.

Haulage Statistics, 1966

Month	Runs	New
Jan	21	7
Feb	47	20
Mar	62	22
Apr	78	32
May	66	26
Jun	60	26
Jul	82	49
Aug	90	51
Sep	111	38
Oct	70	19
Nov	66	15
Dec	84	6
Total	**837**	**311**

GLOSSARY OF ABBREVIATIONS

BR	British Railways
BSK	Brake Second Corridor
DC	Direct Current
DEMU	Diesel-Electric Multiple Unit
DL	Diesel Locomotive
DMO	Divisional Manager's Office
DMU	Diesel Multiple Unit
ECML	East Coast Main Line
ECS	Empty Coaching Stock
EE	English Electric
EL	Electric Locomotive
ELR	East Lancashire Railway
EMU	Electric Multiple Unit
ER	Eastern Region
FO	Friday Only
G&SWR	Glasgow & South Western Railway
GC	Great Central
GWML	Great Western Main Line
GWR	Great Western Railway
K&ESR	Kent & East Sussex Railway
L&NWR	London & North Western Railway
L&SWR	London & South Western Railway
L&YR	Lancashire & Yorkshire Railway
LCGB	Locomotive Club of Great Britain

LMR	London Midland Region
LMS	London, Midland & Scottish
LNER	London & North Eastern Railway
MIC	Mutual Improvement Class
MN	Merchant Navy
MNA	Master Neverers Association
NER	North Eastern Region
NYMR	North Yorkshire Moors Railway
PT&R	Promotion, Transfer and Redundancy
S&D	Somerset & Dorset
SO	Saturdays Only
SR	Southern Region
SX	Saturdays Excepted
TC	Trailer Control
TOPS	Total Operations Processing System
TPO	Travelling Post Office
WC	West Country
WCML	West Coast Main Line
WD	War Department
WR	Western Region

SOURCES

British Rail Database (www.brdatabase.info).

British Rail Main Line: Gradient Profiles (Shepperton: Ian Allen, 1966).

Fuller, Aidan L.F., *British Railways Shed Directory* (several editions).

Locomotive Club of Great Britain, *Bulletin* magazine.

Longworth, Hugh, *BR Steam Locomotives: Complete Allocations History, 1948–1968* (Manchester: Crecy Publishing, 2014).

Six Bells Junction (www.sixbellsjunction.co.uk).

ACKNOWLEDGEMENTS

This book is dedicated to those who made 1966 a year to remember – the co-operative train crews and shed foremen and the many members of the enthusiast fraternity with whom those heady days were spent.

One mustn't overlook the skill of John Bird of ANISTR.com, whose miracles on 50-plus-year-old negatives made them worthy of inclusion here.

Many thanks go to The History Press for putting it all together and, finally, *Steam Days* magazine editor Rex Kennedy, who published my first article in 2004, thus kick-starting a late-life career as an author.

You can view my photographs on www.lorddowding.smugmug.com, where you can click on any of the galleries, set it up for a slide show, sit back and enjoy.

BY THE SAME AUTHOR

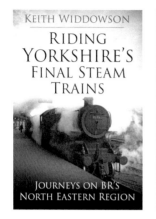

9780750960472

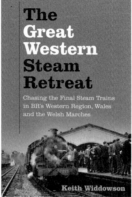

9780750999779

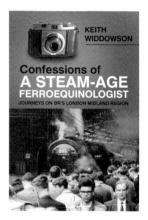

9780750991971

9780750970228

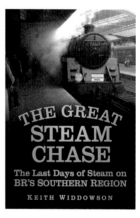

9780752479576

The History Press

The destination for history
www.thehistorypress.co.uk